Teaching Matters

General Editors: Sydney Hill and C

Teaching
Controversial Issues

Robert Stradling, Michael Noctor and Bridget Baines

Curriculum Review Unit, London

Edward Arnold

© Robert Stradling, Michael Noctor and Bridget Baines 1984

First published in Great Britain 1984
by Edward Arnold (Publishers) Ltd
41 Bedford Square
London WC1B 3DQ

Edward Arnold (Australia) Pty Ltd
80 Waverley Road
Caulfield East 3145
PO Box 234
Melbourne

Reprinted 1985

British Library Cataloguing in Publication Data

Stradling, Robert
    Teaching controversial issues.—(Teaching matters)
    1. History, Modern—1945– —Study and teaching
    —Great Britain   2. Social sciences—
    Study and teaching—Great Britain
    I. Title   II. Noctor, Michael
    III. Baines, Bridget   IV. Series
    907'.1041   D842.5

    ISBN 0-7131-0933-5

Text set in 10/11 pt Baskerville
by Keyset Composition, Colchester, Essex
Printed at The Bath Press, Avon

General Editors' Preface

The books in this series provide information and advice on a wide range of educational issues for teachers who are busy, yet who are concerned to keep abreast of new developments.

The aim is practicality: slim volumes that are sources of authoritative help and swift reference, written and edited by people whose expertise in their field is backed up by experience of the everyday realities of school and classroom. The books are planned to cover well-defined topics relevant to schools in widely differing situations: subject teaching, curriculum development, areas of responsibility within schools, and the relationship of the school to the community. They are published at a time when there is a growing call for increased professional accountability in our primary and secondary schools. The 'in-service between covers' that characterizes these handbooks is designed to contribute to the vitality and development of schools and of the individuals within them.

In working with 14–18 year olds, teachers of History and Social Studies, and increasingly of other subjects such as English and Science, are dealing with controversial issues in the classroom. The authors of this book have great experience of working with other teachers in responding to the opportunities and difficulties involved. After discussing what makes an issue controversial they go on to deal with a variety of examples, concentrating on an analysis of a range of possible strategies rather than making universal prescriptions. By studying in turn unemployment, sexism, Northern Ireland, the nuclear debate and the Third World, they raise in one form or another virtually all the problems which are likely to confront the classroom teacher dealing with controversial issues. The result is a book with a wide potential application which is at the same time thought provoking, clear-headed and full of practical ideas.

Acknowledgements

The authors would like to express their thanks to the Leverhulme Trust for funding the research reported in this book. We would also like to acknowledge our debt of gratitude to the following people who helped us greatly and cheerfully tolerated our presence as observers in their classrooms: John Baxter, Geoff Branner, Chris Dickenson, Paddy Doran, Peter Gallie, Ian Gasper, Robin Gildersleeve, Dick Hamblin, David Hunt, Beryl Husain, Dave Kennelly, Bill McDonnell, Rob McGraw, Dave Olroyd, Ian Pearce, Barbara Pepper, Margaret Sandra, Isobel Sheperdson, Bernard Shoreland, John Simpson, John Slater, Judy Tomlinson, John Waddleton, Keith West.

The authors would also like to thank Frauke Hansen for typing and organizing the manuscript.

The publishers would like to thank the following for permission to reproduce copyright material:

Robin Chambers, Annie Cornbleet and Sue Libovith for their 'Anti-sexist/equal opportunities' policy at Clissold Park School, Hackney; Allan Cochrane and Roger Dicker for extracts from a Birmingham Community Development Project report *Workers on the Scrapheap* 1977; Development Education Centre for the web showing global interdependence; Jordanhill Project in International Understanding for a map from *Interdependence*; an extract from an article in *The New Era* volume 60, 1979; *The Teacher* for 'Peace bias claim denied'; Syndication International for the photo on p. 24.

Contents

1

Controversial issues in the classroom

Robert Stradling

Controversial issues in the curriculum

Controversial issues are now an integral and inescapable part of the secondary school curriculum. Over the past twenty years, and particularly since the raising of the school-leaving age to 16, the school curriculum has expanded to include a whole new range of subject areas loosely concerned with preparation for adult life: social, moral, political, careers and sex education, multi-cultural studies, and an assortment of courses such as Design for Living, Personal and Social Development, Community Studies, and Modern Studies. Many of these courses focus on issues and problems either because these are perceived to be highly relevant to students' present and future experiences, or because it is thought that the study of issues is inherently more interesting than the study of institutions or abstract ideas and principles.

Virtually all subjects and disciplines have their controversies and unresolved questions. Historians, for example, disagree over interpretations of events and people's behaviour such as whether Richard III was the evil villain Shakespeare portrayed or a much maligned man. In geography there are competing theories and models of how towns and cities develop. Economists dispute the causes of inflation. Novels and plays set for study in English continue to be a matter of controversy among scholars and critics. The natural sciences also have their fundamental disputes and controversies: the origins of the universe, evolution, the practical application of scientific theories and inventions, the effects of technological advance on the quality of life. To teach these subjects as if there were no controversies or open questions about matters of fact and interpretation would be to mislead students and to misrepresent the nature and the development of academic disciplines and methods of enquiry (1).

The nature of controversy

The term *controversial issue* has already been used a number of times and in slightly different ways, so before going any further some sort of working definition is probably necessary. Often when people say that some topical

theme in a syllabus is controversial they mean that it is politically sensitive. That is, that suspicions, anger or concern may be aroused amongst
some parents, pupils, the school governors or the Local Education
Committee because of the inclusion of the topic in the curriculum or
because of the way in which that topic is being taught. Some of the issues
included in this book (e.g. sexism and nuclear arms and disarmament) are
controversial or politically sensitive in this sense for many schools.

Nevertheless, topics which are politically sensitive in this way for either
the school or the individual teacher need not necessarily be inherently
controversial. For example, there may not be any fundamental disagreements amongst biologists about the functioning of the human body but
the manner in which the teacher demonstrates these functions could well
be politically sensitive. What is a matter for dispute here is not the status
or validity of the subject matter, but rather the teaching methods and the
professionalism of the teacher.

In a sense an issue is controversial 'if numbers of people are observed to
disagree about statements and assertions made in connection with the
issue' (2). They may not be able to agree because there is insufficient
evidence to settle the matter — a state of affairs which is commonplace in
all academic disciplines. Such issues cease to be controversial once
sufficient evidence is forthcoming. Thus, few people would expect geographers to give credence to the claims of the Flat Earth Society. But other
issues are controversial precisely because they are not capable of being
settled by appeal to evidence. These are issues where the disagreement
centres on matters of value judgement. The major political, social and
economic issues of our time or of any previous era tend to be of this type.
As Fraser puts it, they are issues 'for which society has not found a solution
that can be universally or almost universally accepted', and each of the
proposed ways of dealing with them proves objectionable to a significant
section of the community and arouses protest (3).

It is this kind of issue, arising out of a conflict of values, which confronts
the teacher with the most fundamental pedagogic problems. In subsequent chapters we shall therefore focus primarily on issues such as
nuclear disarmament, sexism, Northern Ireland, unemployment and
relations with the Third World, which do embody major conflicts of
values in our society and which also present teachers with considerable
problems in the classroom

Therefore, throughout the rest of this book we have reserved the use of
the term *controversial issue* for those problems and disputes which divide
society and for which significant groups within society offer conflicting
explanations and solutions based on alternative values. Such disputes
may be about:

– what has happened
– the causes of the present situation

  – the desirable ends to work towards
  – the appropriate course of action to be taken
  – the likely effects of that action.

With some issues there may be disagreement about all of these things.
Northern Ireland would seem to be a case in point. With other issues (for
example, unemployment) there may be consensus about ends but disagreement about causes and appropriate solutions.

The more contemporary the issue the greater the problems for the
teacher, mainly because the outcome may still be very difficult to predict:
we do not have the benefit of hindsight regarding the significance of recent
events; students are likely to bring with them into the classroom their own
interpretations, experiences, judgements and prejudices; the primary
sources of evidence are likely to be biased, incomplete and contradictory;
and it is even difficult to establish criteria for determining what does and
does not constitute valid evidence.

Why teach controversial issues?

This may seem a paradoxical question given the earlier point that controversial issues are an integral and inescapable part of the school
curriculum. However, I have raised this question at this point to draw
attention to the fact that teachers include controversial issues in their
courses for very different reasons and that sometimes these reasons can
have implications for the way in which they teach such issues.

Some teachers include controversial issues in their teaching because
they are topical and may be directly relevant to students' lives, or because
they are major social, political, economic or moral problems of our time
and consequently aspects of life which students ought to know something
about. Others concentrate on issues which, as Lawrence Stenhouse puts
it, are 'matters of widespread and enduring significance' which, if
neglected, would leave a serious gap in the child's education (**4**). Themes
dealing with such issues often concentrate on relationships between the
sexes, the distribution of scarce resources in society, work, war and peace,
law and order, and so forth. These various approaches have one thing in
common. The issues are taught because it is thought that they deal with
matters which students should know something about and understand;
that is, the issues are taught for their own sake and as ends in themselves.
For the sake of convenience I shall refer to such approaches as *product-based*.

The justification for a product-based approach is clear enough, but the
potential problems should not be overlooked. Many contemporary issues
are highly complex. A comprehensive understanding of such issues (e.g.
crime and punishment) might well require at least some knowledge of the
economic, sociological, political, historical and psychological factors
involved. This puts considerable demands on the resources of the teacher.

One solution may be team teaching but for many schools it would seem that the organizational constraints inhibiting the introduction of team teaching are proving insurmountable. Another alternative might be for teachers to eschew the role of knowledgeable experts and opt instead for teaching through enquiry-based learning. The potential problem here, however, may be that because the issues are so contemporary it is difficult to obtain teaching materials which deal with these disputes adequately or in a suitably balanced way. Product-based approaches to teaching issues have also been criticized on the grounds that students are often being taught about issues which may be topical and relevant now but may not be so in five years. Consequently such knowledge may be of little use to students later in their adult lives and may be regarded as just one more piece of information quickly forgotten when the student passes through the school gates for the last time.

The alternative proposed by such critics is a *process-based* approach. In this case the issue focused upon is seen as a means to some other end; the issue is regarded as less important than the manner in which it is examined. Teachers adopting this approach may include issues in their courses:

i)   because they offer a useful focus for helping students to develop academic and study skills (for instance, constructing hypotheses, collecting and evaluating evidence, analysing statistics, presenting findings);

ii)   because they offer a useful context for practising social and life skills (for instance, skills in communicating with others, exercising empathy and understanding, influencing others, co-operating in projects, and so forth);

iii) because specific issues may prove to be useful case studies for comprehending theories, concepts and generalizations (for example, the politics of Northern Ireland may be studied not because this is thought to be a major issue of public significance but because it is a useful case study for understanding a theory or model of political and religious conflict).

Essentially the justification for the process-based approach to teaching issues is that whilst specific issues are often transient and ephemeral, and knowledge of them dates quickly and soon becomes irrelevant, the skills and conceptual framework learned through carefully examining selected issues may remain, continue to be of use to students, and form the basis for developing new skills and new concepts. In our experience the main potential problem with the process-based approach is that it is rather difficult for the teacher to gauge its success. It is easier to assess the knowledge gained from teaching about a specific issue than it is to assess the student's capacity to transfer the skills and understanding acquired from looking at one issue on to another. The problem can be further compounded if students are not really clear about the overall purpose of the learning activities they are involved in. Life for some students here can often seem to be an endless series of task cards, work sheets and exercises, and students may feel as if they are driving in a fog, unaware of the direction they are taking.

Process-based and product-based approaches are not necessarily mutually exclusive and clearly some syllabuses are designed to teach a product (knowledge and understanding of issues) while also developing certain generalizable skills and concepts. But here, too, there are potential pitfalls and problems. Take for example the case of a humanities teacher with a large, mixed-ability class aiming to develop analytical skills (particularly the skills of the historian) through an enquiry-based approach and choosing to focus on Northern Ireland because of its topicality and relevance to contemporary life in Britain. Because of its size and range of abilities the class is divided into small groups, each of which focuses on a specific aspect of the issue and reports to the others. This may mean that all pupils get the opportunity to exercise some of the requisite skills of the historian, but possibly at the cost of pupils developing a rather partial and incomplete understanding of the issue.

I have not raised these various problems with the object of persuading you that there is some better alternative that will be revealed in the course of this book. The preference of all three contributors is for some kind of process-based approach to teaching issues which would provide students with a conceptual framework, skills in discussion and a critical, analytical approach to events and public disagreements in order that they can transfer these on to issues and situations which they will encounter later in their adult lives. However, we do not underestimate the difficulties of such an approach. Nevertheless, the problems we have briefly alluded to above (and which will be dealt with in more detail when looking at specific issues later in this book) may not arise for all teachers or may be effectively circumvented. This is why we emphasize that they are only *potential* problems.

Teaching strategies and methods

The starting-point for any discussion of how to teach issues is undoubt-edly the role of the teacher in the classroom. Three concepts seem to be central to this: balance, neutrality and commitment.

Balance

When asked how the teacher should approach controversial issues, many headteachers, local authority advisers and even chief education officers stress the importance of presenting students with a balanced picture. By this they appear to mean that the teacher should offer students a range of alternative viewpoints on each issue. But balance is a deceptively simple concept which on further examination raises a number of difficult questions.

Firstly, is it necessary to have a balanced approach to every single lesson or can one think instead in terms of a balanced approach across a unit or module of lessons, or even across an overall course, whereby the teacher ensures that by the end of a school term or year the student has encountered a range of alternatives but not necessarily in each lesson?

Second, what is more important here: balanced teaching or balanced learning? In the areas of the curriculum where controversial issues predominate the teacher is in a very different position to, say, the physics or mathematics teacher. We are not initiating the students into a body of knowledge with which they are totally unfamiliar. We are intervening in a learning process which is well underway before they do any humanities or social studies. They bring with them into the classroom their own experiences, knowledge, commitments and prejudices. So, as teachers, do we ignore all of this extra-mural learning from family, peers and the mass media and offer students instead a balanced spectrum of views, including those to which they are already committed, or do we, for example, play the 'devil's advocate'? Do we seek to present them with an alternative point of view to their own at all times (even if it is a view to which we ourselves are not committed)? This, too, might be said to be a balanced approach but can clearly present teachers with problems if some students (and their parents) assume that the views presented by the teacher as devil's advocate are their own.

Finally, when considering a balanced approach it is also necessary to consider carefully whether we are talking about a genuine spectrum of alternative viewpoints or are limiting ourselves to those viewpoints which are generally accepted within, say, the broad consensus of liberal-democratic values or even the liberal-humanist ideology that pervades so much educational theory in Britain. So, for example, in political education one might argue that students should have an opportunity to examine critically not only the policies of Labour, the Conservatives, the Liberals and the Social Democrats but also the National Front and British Movement, the Socialist Workers Party and the Communist Party. On the other hand, many parents might find the inclusion of the ideas and policies of some of these parties wholly unacceptable. It may also be the case that teaching about such policies might prove potentially divisive within the school if, for instance, it is situated in a multi-ethnic community. As a teacher you might also fear that the airing of certain very extreme positions on such matters as immigration will do no more than reinforce students' prejudices (5). In some circumstances, there may still be strong grounds for going ahead and presenting all points of view, however extreme or potentially divisive.

We raise questions about the balanced approach here simply because we doubt that balance can ever be regarded as a kind of guiding educational principle to be followed regardless of circumstance or constraints operating in a particular school, or regardless of students' reactions to the approach. The journalist, James Cameron, made a telling point about the potential problems of a balanced approach when he took issue with the Independent Broadcasting Association's decision not to screen the television programme *The Truth Game* on the nuclear arms race until it could be balanced by a second programme advocating the other point of view. "What is this 'balance'? Roget defines it as 'equality, parity, co-extension, symmetry, level, monotony'. How do you achieve the first five of these qualities without dropping into the sixth?" (**6**).

Neutrality

In the teaching of controversial issues, perhaps the concept of neutrality is now most closely associated with the Humanities Curriculum Project (HCP). Starting from the assumption that 'the authority position of the teacher is much stronger than most teachers realize, and that it is almost insuperably difficult for him to put forward his own points of view without implying that controversial issues can be settled on the basis of the authority of others', the project team opted for *procedural neutrality* in the classroom. This involved adopting a strategy in which the teacher's role is that of an impartial chairman of discussion groups, ensuring that all students can have their say, treating their opinions consistently, feeding in evidence when needed, and avoiding the assertion of his or her own preferences and allegiances (**7**).

The HCP teaching strategy has been characterized as follows:

1.   The fundamental educational values of rationality, imagination, sensitivity, readiness to listen to the views of others, and so forth must be built into the principles of procedure in the classroom.
2.   The pattern of teaching must renounce the authority of the teacher as an 'expert' capable of solving value issues since this authority cannot be justified either epistemologically or politically. In short, the teacher must aspire to be neutral.
3.   The teaching strategy must maintain the procedural authority of the teacher in the classroom, but contain it within rules which can be justified in terms of the need for discipline and rigour in attaining understanding.
4.   The strategy must be such as to satisfy parents and pupils that every possible effort is being made to avoid the use of the teacher's authority position to indoctrinate his/her own views.
5.   The procedure must enable pupils to understand divergence of views and hence must depend upon a group working together through discussion and shared activities. In such a group

opinions should be respected, and minority opinions should be protected from ridicule or from social pressure.

6. In sensitive issues, thought must be given to preserving privacy and protecting students.

7. Above all, the aim should be understanding. This implies that one should not force pupils towards opinions or premature commitments which harden into prejudice. Nor should one see particular virtue in a change of view. The object is that the pupil should come to understand the nature and implications of his/ her own personal view and be accountable for it. Whether or not the pupil changes his/her point of view is not significant for the attainment of understanding (**7**).

The whole raison d'être for procedural neutrality is that teachers occupy a position of authority over their students and therefore any views they express will carry extra weight and influence the children. At present there is very little research evidence either to support or invalidate this assumption. In 1969 Miller, working with day-release students in Further Education, found that using a wide range of teaching methods to combat racial prejudice tended, if anything, to increase rather than reduce the students' prejudices (**5**). More recently, Stenhouse and Verma evaluated the use of three different strategies (neutral chairman, committed approach and teaching through drama) for teaching race relations and concluded that some students will become less racist and some will become more racist regardless of method (**8**). Students are not tabulae rasae. Many attitudes and prejudices are formed early in life and are well established before children enter secondary schools. Furthermore, many such prejudices are strongly reinforced at home and amongst friends, groups which often have more authority with children and teenagers than their teachers.

The original HCP team also seemed to assume that the only alternative to the role of neutral chairman is that of instructor. Thus Stenhouse asserts, 'The basic classroom pattern should be one of discussion. Instruction inevitably implies that the teacher cannot maintain a neutral position' (**7**). This rather simplistic distinction fails to take account of a whole range of student-centred and resource-based methods of learning including projects, field work, analysis of case studies and even role play and simulation, as well as other ways of organizing discussion (e.g. in small groups).

The assumption that discussion led by a neutral chairman ensures that pupils will consider and understand a divergence of views is also questionable. What does the teacher do if this divergence of opinion is missing in classroom discussion? What, for example, does the teacher do when faced by unquestioning consensus from the entire class? Indeed, the HCP seems to recognize this problem at one point and admits that on occasion the teacher may have to 'represent a view which the group has not considered' in order to challenge awareness of complacency (**7**). Such situations are by no means a rarity in the classroom and adopting the role of devil's advocate can be a highly effective counter to it, but it should be emphasized that it is a very different role from that of neutral chairman.

Commitment

When is it legitimate for a teacher to state his or her own commitments and allegiances in the classroom, and is it ever acceptable to go beyond this and consistently teach in a committed way? There are a number of points for discussion here. The first is essentially procedural.

Stenhouse, in explaining the thinking of HCP, asserts that they are not advocating a value-free approach but that the values they wish to uphold are educational rather than substantive or partisan ones. Some teachers, however, reject the possibility of maintaining an impartial line on substantive values. Underpinning their position is the assumption that they will lose credibility with pupils if they do not say what they think, particularly when asked. One might also add that stating your own commitments and allegiances gives students a chance to make allowance for your 'prejudices and opinions' when evaluating what you say and how you tackle the issue.

A second point raised by some teachers is that there are some issues on which you cannot be impartial. This is an approach that derives from a view of education as being more than just learning *about* the social world. Education is seen here as being also concerned with helping students to develop strategies and skills for influencing social change. Other teachers take a similar line but are primarily concerned with individual attitude change. This often applies to attitudes towards race, sexism and in particular, the understanding that should be shown towards social and sexual minorities. Even teachers of relatively non-controversial areas of the curriculum such as health education often appear to be committed to attitude and behavioural change on such matters as drug-taking, glue-sniffing, alcoholism and cigarette-smoking.

Third, there is the view that a committed approach challenges students to think, to clarify their own point of view, to become aware of the contradictions and inconsistencies in their thinking, and to sort out fact from value-judgement.

Indoctrination

Whatever the justification for a committed approach to teaching issues, the main potential problem inevitably is the risk of indoctrination or, at least, the risk of allegations of indoctrination. This raises a number of questions, some of which will be dealt with in a later chapter, some of which can at least be clarified if not answered, and some of which can only be answered by each individual reader. For example, is all committed teaching the same as indoctrination or can some of it be justified on educational grounds?

Indoctrination is usually associated with attempts to teach something as if it were true or universally acceptable regardless of evidence to the contrary or in the absence of any evidence at all (**9**). On this basis, teachers who make their own positions clear when teaching about issues need not necessarily be indoctrinating:

   i)   if other points of view receive fair and equal treatment;
   ii) if the teacher is simply attempting to redress the balance by stating a point of view which is different from the one propounded by the child's main source of information and opinion — the mass media;
   iii) if the teacher encourages students to subject his or her own point of view to critical examination;
   iv) if the teacher is expressing his or her own point of view to challenge pupils' own unquestioned assumptions and attitudes.

Under some circumstances the ethics of one or more of these objectives might be questionable, also in some circumstances one or more of these objectives might prove objectionable to parents, but as long as students are not being asked to accept statements at face value or to treat value judgements as if they were facts, then the teacher is not indoctrinating them.

Two other questions then arise which we will leave open for now and return to later when we have looked at more examples of classroom practice on specific issues. These are:

   i)   Are teachers indoctrinating if the point of view they express is already shared by most or all of their students?
   ii) Are there some beliefs and values which are so important, so central to the well-being of the individual or the community that it is legitimate for schools to inculcate them through indoctrination?

The latter is probably a question which each teacher, school or LEA must decide on individually. We have already suggested that some schools do consciously inculcate certain attitudes and beliefs, and seek to change specific attitudes. The examples from health education are fairly typical. Some schools have a policy against racism as do some local education authorities, and an increasing number of schools are now developing a policy on sexism. In such cases teachers are expected to take a committed line against the manifestations of both racism and sexism. When we ask headteachers about the educational implications of such policies they often point out that it is legitimate for schools to counter racist or sexist attitudes and behaviour because there is legislation against both racial and sexual discrimination. In the absence of legislative legitimacy presumably schools would have to rely on some other form of external authority for teaching issues in a committed way, such as 'the national consensus': a rather more nebulous and unsatisfactory criterion in a pluralist society. However, this criterion is applied in some schools, particularly regarding controversial issues in religious and moral education and also in sex and health education.

In this discussion of all three concepts (balance, neutrality and commitment) there has been a recurring question: are they educational principles or simply teaching strategies which may or may not be useful for handling controversial issues? The advocates of balance, neutrality or commitment tend to assume that they are basic principles. The teachers we have talked to and our own classroom experience suggest that they are not. It all depends on the circumstances one encounters in the classroom. If students have a lot to say, if there is a broad spread of opinion, and if their views are based on knowledge and experience rather than blind prejudice, then there is a good case for adopting the role of neutral chairman. In other circumstances the balanced or committed approaches might be more appropriate.

It simply is not possible to lay down hard-and-fast rules about teaching controversial subject matter to be applied at all times. The teacher has to take account of the knowledge, values and experiences which the students bring with them into the classroom; the teaching methods which predominate in other lessons; the classroom climate (e.g. unquestioning consensus, apathy, or polarization of opinion); and the age and ability of the students. But, above all, in teaching controversial issues the teacher has to be highly responsive to the reactions of pupils both to the content of lessons and the teaching methods being employed. Any controversial issue can arouse strong emotions leading to a polarization of the class and consequent hostility. On the other hand, even with issues which may divide the entire nation, teachers can find themselves confronted by a wall of apathy or alienation, or unquestioning consensus, and so on. These different circumstances in the classroom require different methods and strategies and there is no guarantee that a strategy which works with one set of pupils will necessarily work with another group.

In the following chapters, therefore, the authors have deliberately eschewed universal prescriptions for teaching issues. They have drawn on their own experiences and the experiences of teachers with whom they have been working in order to present a range of alternative approaches to teaching a specific issue. The potential strengths and weaknesses of the various options are discussed in the light of the sorts of constraints referred to earlier in this chapter. So, for example, Chapter Four highlights the different constraints which operate in the coeducational school compared with a single-sex school when teachers introduce lessons on sexual discrimination and sexism. Chapter Three suggests that when deciding how to tackle the issue of unemployment teachers should take into account the prevailing types of unemployment in their locality, particularly in those jobs which have been traditional sources of employment for school leavers.

In certain respects Chapters Three and Four differ from the others in so far as they have ramifications for the school which far outweigh the problems of teaching a controversial topic within an established school course or syllabus. The issue of sexism, for example, raises contentious questions about the hidden curriculum, staff relations, teacher-pupil relations, and the possibility of a whole-school policy. What a school chooses to do about youth unemployment — whether it teaches *about* it or prepares young people *for* it, or both — raises questions which are educationally as well as politically controversial. By comparison, issues relating to Northern Ireland, the Third World or nuclear weapons are more straightforward. Consequently Chapters Two, Five and Six are essentially concerned with the teacher's approach to the content, the styles of teaching and teaching methods used.

However, it should also be emphasized that each issue presents its own unique problems for the teacher. As the introduction to Chapter Two points out, in most controversial issues the conflict focuses on one or two aspects of the issue. People agree about the ultimate goal but disagree about the methods of getting there; or they agree about the causes of a particular problem but disagree about the solutions to it. With Northern Ireland we have a controversial issue in which the various conflicting parties disagree at every level of the issue, i.e. about the causes of the situation, the effects, the policies and solutions or even the ultimate goal for policy.

In any book on teaching controversial issues there are likely to be some glaring omissions. Some readers might have expected chapters on such issues as racism, crime or industrial relations. To some extent we avoided these issues because we felt that they had been thoroughly dealt with elsewhere — there is, for example, a burgeoning industry on teaching about racism. But we also felt that the issues which we finally decided to include here raise in one form or another virtually all the teaching problems which are likely to confront the classroom teacher dealing with controversial issues. They are also issues which increasingly appear in social studies, general studies and humanities courses in middle and secondary schools, and in various modules in further education courses.

2

Teaching about Northern Ireland

Michael Noctor

Controversial issues that are dealt with in schools are often transient. For example, the invasion and subsequent war in the Falkland Islands in 1982 was the subject of heated debate in many classrooms throughout the country at the time. The issue was short-lived and it would be surprising indeed to find many schools still dealing with it today. By contrast, the problems of Northern Ireland have been in the public's attention for the past fifteen years and show no signs of being resolved in the near future. News reports appear regularly and present a fragmented and confusing picture of a highly complex issue.

This issue differs from some others (such as nuclear weapons, where everyone wants to prevent nuclear war but disagrees as to how this can best be done) in that there is no agreement about what a desirable outcome to the present conflict would be. Some advocate that Northern Ireland should remain part of the United Kingdom, others that it should form part of a United Ireland, and others that it should become an independent state.

The gulf between the Unionist and Nationalist traditions is so wide that there exist no criteria for discussing events and options or deciding which questions should be on the agenda, which would satisfy the various groups involved. There is disagreement at a number of different levels concerning what has happened in the past, the significance of various factors in contributing to the present situation, what the outcome ought to be and what constitutes acceptable political activity. Thus discussion of questions concerning the relationship of Northern Ireland to Great Britain and the Republic of Ireland, the legitimacy of the state, the role of the armed forces, and the use of violence for political purposes can be highly emotive.

For many teachers the reason for dealing with Northern Ireland in the classroom is self-evident: it is a major contemporary and enduring issue which pupils ought to know something about and which bears directly or indirectly on their lives. It is an issue which often appears in political education, social studies and modern history syllabuses because it has major implications for our understanding of parliamentary democracy and civil rights. Other teachers, however, would use this issue primarily as a case study, useful for developing transferable process skills of the type discussed in Chapter One.

Teaching problems

Whatever the rationale for dealing with Northern Ireland as an issue, teachers are likely to confront three major problems:

1. Children develop political attitudes at an early age as a result of coming into contact with a range of different sources of information and opinion including family and friends and the mass media, as well as school. Research on the political awareness of young people has shown a remarkable degree of ignorance of political matters. Perhaps one of the most disturbing findings of this research was that 44 per cent of the fifteen-year-olds in a national survey thought that 'the IRA is a Protestant organization set up to prevent Ulster from being united with the rest of Ireland' (**1**).

2. Information concerning events and the motives of people involved is often contradictory and incomplete. Access to sources outside the bounds of the 'national consensus' tends to be restricted. It is difficult, and in some cases illegal, to obtain the views of para-military groups, whether Loyalist or Republican. Such views rarely receive coverage in the mass media. Similarly much of the official view (for example, army reports on the strengths and weaknesses of para-military organizations or on the extent and nature of covert operations) is not available to the public on grounds of security. Research has shown that the selection and presentation of news coverage by television news gives weight to the orthodox view of events, preventing 'the alternative perspective surfacing in anything more than a fragmentary and incoherent way' (**2**).

3. Events and disputes such as the use of plastic bullets, bombings and hunger strikes arouse strong emotions in classroom discussion. Even so, it may often be the case that interest is low until violence spills over onto the mainland. Depending on circumstances then, the teacher may be faced with the problem of widespread apathy about the issue or widespread anger. Northern Ireland has never ranked very high in opinion polls dealing with the 'most important issue' for people in Great Britain (**3**). Yet in an opinion poll, conducted after the hunger strike of 1981, only 6 per cent of those questioned about the presence of British troops in Northern Ireland did not have an opinion, while 37 per cent believed that the troops should be removed immediately (**3**). It is an area, then, where one can encounter in any group of people ignorance, apathy and strong emotions and attitudes.

Decisions concerning how to teach this issue should involve consideration of the problems mentioned above, the context in which the teaching takes place and the aims of the teaching. For example, teaching pupils who come predominantly from army families may require an approach which initially distances them from the problems of Northern Ireland by using parallels and then subsequently moves on to examine events in the Province. On the other hand, teaching pupils who have no direct experience or interest requires more thought on how best to motivate them.

Four ways of dealing with this issue are outlined below. In some cases a combination of these approaches may be more appropriate than using any one approach exclusively as in many ways they complement each other. So, for example, where the problems are ignorance and an unquestioning consensus amongst the pupils, a combination of media analysis and an historical account of the policies and events leading up to the present conflict may be useful. On the other hand where the problem is one of entrenched attitudes and prejudices coupled with some selective knowledge, it may be that an approach which combined empathizing and enquiry skills would prove more successful.

Contexts and approaches

Historical approach

Northern Ireland provides an interesting illustration of a 'historical' issue in so far as the people of the Province have a highly developed awareness of their own history. For them the problem is not interpreted purely in contemporary terms: the wealth of songs and celebrations which commemorate particular historical events testifies to this. Indeed it is difficult to imagine how a discussion of the issue could avoid historical considerations, or how pupils could acquire a thorough understanding of the current troubles in Northern Ireland if they themselves lacked a historical perspective. Undoubtedly, the present situation is made more comprehensible by exploring the significance of events, ideas, trends and movements within a historical framework which focuses on change and continuity and encourages speculation about causes and consequences.

However, the history of Ireland is long, complex and highly disputed. How far back does one go? Should one, for example, start with the Norman invasion of 1169 headed by the Earl of Pembroke (known as Strongbow)? Or the Plantations policy initiated during the early seventeenth century? Or the storming and sacking of Drogheda by Cromwell in 1549? Or the war between James II and William of Orange and the Battle of the Boyne in 1691? Or the Society of United Irishmen and the abortive rising of 1798? Or should the starting-point be later with, for example, the Home Rule movement of the 1880s? Or the Easter Rising of 1916? Or the Partitioning of Ireland in 1920 and the subsequent Civil

War? Or would the appropriate starting-point be the Civil Rights
Movement of the 1960s?

Any attempt at a historical understanding involves a process of
selection in deciding which events carry most significance and which are
of little importance. While the historian will have to judge this selection on
the basis of historical criteria, the teacher needs to consider the starting
points of the pupils. In this sense the history teacher will take into account
the prejudices, misconceptions, knowledge and attitudes of the pupils
when deciding which events to focus upon. In many cases it is necessary to
introduce some doubt in the minds of pupils by examining events which
do not comply with a simplistic view of the issue. For example, if one is
teaching a group of children of Irish Catholic parents who hold predominantly Republican views it may prove useful to point out that the founding
figure of Irish Republicanism, Theobald Wolfe Tone, was in fact a
Protestant. Similarly, it would be useful to explore the different traditions
of Republicanism both constitutional and non-constitutional and how
these relate to the current situation, as a way of unravelling the complexities of such concepts of Republicanism and of debunking the simple
view that all Catholics are Republican and Republicans are Catholic.

Given the politically sensitive nature of the Northern Ireland issue, an
approach which seeks a detached, academic treatment may provide a way
of circumventing accusations of bias while leaving the professional
credibility of the teacher intact. At its best the traditional history
approach provides pupils with a range of perspectives and knowledge
concerning the background to the troubles and a conceptual framework.
However, there are a number of potential problems with this approach.

First, deciding which events to concentrate on as being central to an
understanding of an issue will in itself involve covert bias even if the
individual events are dealt with in a balanced way. The danger is that in
trying to avoid accusations of bias the misleading impression may be
given that history can be value-free.

Second, given the constraints of time, this approach sometimes appears
to present pupils with refined, polished and seamless accounts of the past.
This may lead them to feel that the way in which the history of Northern
Ireland has developed is inevitable.

Third, there is the danger that pupils will not appreciate that
historical accounts are actually constructions and interpretations made
on the basis of limited evidence and within an ideological and episte-
mological framework. As such they are always open to question to a
greater or lesser degree. Shemilt, the evaluator of the Schools Council
History 13-16 Project, found that the pupils on traditional history courses
tended to see history as a corpus of 'pre-existent, pre-digested and
inalienable facts. These facts were construed as absolutely true and
absolutely unchanging' (4). This is a particular problem with a contemporary issue such as Northern Ireland where certain historical

constructions coincide with current political ideologies.

Finally, in dealing with this issue over a short period, there may be a temptation to reduce events to a logical progression which may in turn lead to seeing developments as inevitable and to ignoring the significance of current events in shaping the future of Northern Ireland. It seems unlikely that a historical approach of this sort could adequately provide a comprehensive understanding of such a complex and multi-faceted issue. The development of such an understanding would seem to require a consideration of contemporary political, economic, and sociological factors as well as the historical dimension. Perhaps I can best illustrate this point by raising the following question. To what extent was the rise of the Civil Rights Movement in Ulster in 1968 the result solely of historical antecedents and to what extent was it influenced by contemporary developments such as the growth of students' and civil rights movements in the United States and Western Europe?

Schools Council History 13–16 Project: 'The Irish Question'

This project was in many ways a response to what were seen to be the inadequacies of traditional history teaching. The first part of the course is designed to introduce pupils to the nature of history and to explore the types of skills which are central to the discipline. The second part of the course contains four Modern World Studies options: The Arab–Israeli Conflict; The Rise of Communist China; The Irish Question; and The Move to European Unity. Two of these topics have to be covered.

The aims of 'The Irish Question' are twofold:

a) to develop an understanding of this topic by exploring it in its historical context;
b) to provide experience in the analysis of evidence.

Underpinning these aims are the assumptions that '. . . the burning issues and problems of the contemporary world cannot be understood in ignorance of their antecedents' and that historical explanation is not the same as explanation in natural science, as it '. . . usually amounts to a reduction of uncertainty, rarely to an impeccable solution' (4).

As 'The Irish Question' falls into the second part of the course, considerable work will have preceded it concerning the use of analytical skills for dealing with evidence. It is recommended that in introducing the study the teacher starts by dealing with the latest news about Ireland using newspaper cuttings and recordings of television and radio programmes where possible. The purpose of this is to identify the important aspects of the current situation in order to explore the factors involved in the background to this situation. The materials available for use with this topic include a pupil's book, a tape recordng and a filmstrip.

The themes dealt with in the pupil's book are:

The origins of the two communities
The Protestant ascendancy
The struggle for Home Rule
Civil War and the treaty
Divisions in Northern Ireland since 1921
Why is the Irish Question a world issue?

While exploring these themes it is not thought necessary that all the sources should be examined in equal detail. In selecting sources, however, the project team emphasize that '. . . 1) equal weight is given to the bias of all parties to the conflict; 2) a partisan account of an incident is checked against an official account, where possible' (5). Having made the first stipulation it seems rather odd to assume that official accounts will necessarily be more authoritative.

The strength of this approach lies in its attempt to show how historians (and by implication other people such as contemporary observers, journalists, etc.) construct and reconstruct historical reality. Taxing though this approach is or can be, it does provide experience of critically assessing evidence which is likely to be of use to pupils when they examine other issues and may well engender a good deal more healthy scepticism about 'the evidence' put before them than the more traditional approach to history teaching.

The course is aimed at the academically able pupils who will be sitting CSE and GCE 'O' level examinations. Consequently the materials are not designed for less literate students; however, it appears that even for the examination groups the large amount of material is likely to cause some problems (4).

Even so, this kind of approach with its emphasis on the learning process and analytical skills rather than the direct transmission of knowledge, has scope beyond the teaching of history. The strategy for looking at 'The Irish Question' outlined by the project team could just as readily be adopted by social studies teachers or history teachers contributing to broader humanities programmes.

The process of selecting the relevant from the irrelevant is not just a key historical skill; it is also a central skill in developing political literacy or an understanding of society and how it functions. However, it is a skill which needs to be practised by the pupil rather than performed in advance of the lesson by the teacher or, as in this case, by the project team, as this process often involves an implicit bias.

For example, compare the two lists of events below concerning the way in which hostilities grew between the Catholic and Protestant communities between 1968 and the mid-70s. The list on the left is taken from the project's document 'The Irish Question' (6). On the right-hand side I have listed a few other incidents and events which might lead to a different view of the issue. The list on the left tends to present an official and often Loyalist perspective. The overwhelming impression gained here is that the primary problem has been violent activity by Republicans. Contrast this with the list on the right which sees the problem essentially as one of discrimination against the Catholic community and Loyalist intransigence and reaction to events.

How Protestant and Catholic hostility grew after 1968

1968	* The Long March from Belfast to Derry; the fight at Burntollet Bridge	* Growth of campaign protesting at discrimination against Catholics
1969	* British troops called in to help restore order	* Battle of Bogside * Disbandment of the B specials * UVF organized explosions at public meetings
1971	* Republican Movement split * Internment introduced following increase in violence	
1972	* Direct Rule	* Protestant para-military organizations mobilized * Bloody Sunday
1974	* Stormont suspended * Sunningdale agreement	* Ulster Workers Council Strike * End of Political Status for prisoners

The primary and secondary evidence in the pupil's book on 'The Irish Question' is selected and then structured for the pupil both chronologically and thematically. The sources are also contextualized by the narrative in such a way that the book often reads like a text book.

Perhaps what is called for here is an even more thoroughgoing resource-based approach than that offered by the Schools Council project. Genuine opportunities need to be provided for pupils to examine first-hand evidence that has not been previously interpreted, sorted and structured for them. This will give them an insight into how much of the information presented to them by politicians, pressure groups, journalists and others representing vested interests is highly selective, structured and organized to support a particular point of view. Such presentations commonly offer simplistic explanations reducing complex issues into black-and-white terms and often employing emotionally loaded and biased language to serve a particular purpose.

Media analysis

Over the last couple of decades much critical attention has been directed to the way the mass media operate and particularly to how news and current affairs are constructed and portrayed. This attention has been reflected by a growth of interest in media education in various forms in schools (**7**). The way in which media education appears in the curriculum can vary from full courses or modules in media studies to being an integral part of courses whose main focus is some other subject area. What follows is a discussion of an approach to media education which, by using Northern Ireland as a case study, explores current affairs and news reporting in a critical way.

The starting-point for this approach is the view that: i) the mass media is the major source of information for most people on this issue; ii) the information it provides is constructed, and so offers an interpretation of events rather than an objective or neutral account of them. There exists, concerning Northern Ireland, a vast array of competing definitions of the problems there, as well as a range of different solutions. This diversity is not reflected by the way in which the media treat the issue. As Simon Hoggart, a *Guardian* journalist, points out:

> Most journalists working in Northern Ireland are almost completely dependent on this (army) information service (and a smaller one by the police), simply because there is no other source of news of day-to-day violence. This means that the army has an immense advantage of getting the first word, and it is left up to the integrity of the journalist to check that word . . . When the British press prints an account of an incident as if it were an established fact, and it is clear that the reporter himself (sic) is not on the spot, it is a 99 per cent certainty that it is the army's version that is being given (**8**).

Apart from the sources of information journalists use there are other factors which influence the way that current affairs and news are put together. These include: practical constraints involved in obtaining images and sound of reasonable quality; commercial considerations such as which stories sell papers or attract viewers and which do not; and potential legal and political pressures such as the laws of libel and the Official Secrets Act. These factors influence the climate of opinion within the media such that many decisions concerning the production of news and current affairs operate in an implicit fashion to shape how these events are then portrayed.

The sharp divergence of opinion concerning developments in Northern Ireland means that the issue provides a good case study with which to explore the points raised above. Perhaps more importantly for teachers, however, are practical considerations about the availability of resources.

As the issue is both topical and long-running it provides up-to-date material, such as the latest press or radio reports, as well as published critiques of reporting in this area (**9**).

It is central to this approach that pupils learn 'to read between the lines'. Consequently the teaching and learning activities employed usually involve pupils in exercising analytical skills so that they can evaluate the media's treatment of controversial issues. As this requires a degree of sophistication on the part of the pupils, and because of the strong emotions and attitudes that are often involved in classroom discussions about Northern Ireland, it may be necessary initially to employ exercises which are both simple and uncontroversial as a way into the case study. I have outlined below some of the methods that are used by teachers adopting this approach.

Introductory activities

1   A dispute is enacted, after which members of the class adopt different roles (such as the protagonists, friends of the protagonists and someone trying to sell the story). By comparing the different reports, questions can be raised concerning the types of criteria we employ when judging evidence and the extent to which taken-for-granted assumptions condition our selection and presentation of evidence.

2   The use of photographs to convey meaning can be explored by getting the pupils to act as editors in deciding which of a range of photographs best go with the particular 'news story' and what modifications might enhance/detract from the presentation. Published sources (**10**) can be used for this, alternatively it is possible to collect a number of photographs from newspapers relating to the same issue (for example, CND protest marches). The underlying idea here is to raise questions about the criteria employed both when the photograph is taken (such as the angle of the shot and the nature of the subject matter) and when it is selected and modified for use (such as the framing of the picture and the relationship between the different elements in the photograph).

3   When the opportunity permits, it is a useful exercise for pupils to be present at an event that is likely to receive media coverage (such as a local demonstration, strike or appearance by a visiting dignitary). By then reporting on the event themselves and comparing their recollections with the local media treatment of it, the similarities and differences as well as the probable reasons for them can be explored.

Such activities prepare the ground for a case study of Northern Ireland or any other issue where information is itself controversial and open to question and where pupils lack any direct experience to help them make judgements.

The case study
There are a number of general questions which need to be borne in mind
when undertaking case studies of the media treatment of an issue. Such
questions can be raised when appropriate but in order to gain some
overview of the media's treatment it is probably advisable to explore them
in a comparative way. An examination of different newspapers provides a
fairly practical way of doing this. It is relatively easy to obtain copies of
Irish provincial and national newspapers in areas with an Irish community, and these often provide a marked contrast with British newspapers in their treatment of the issue. Similarly *The Irish Post*, which caters
for the Irish community in Britain and is readily available throughout the
country, provides a different perspective from the national British press in
its treatment of events in Northern Ireland. For example, during the
hunger strike of 1981 it regularly gave coverage of how the event was seen
in other parts of the world, informing its readers, for instance, that a street
in Tehran had been named after Bobby Sands, and that the hunger strike
had been debated in the Parliaments of India and Portugal.

In addition to the comparative perspective other aspects of the media's
treatment of Northern Ireland could be examined. Questions to be considered with a class of pupils might include:

1   How are the boundaries of consensus defined and which
    perspectives are included within them and which are excluded?
    With the issue of Northern Ireland the boundaries tend to be
    clearly and narrowly defined. One has to look long and hard for
    an exposition of the case for a United Ireland.
2   What priority is given to Northern Ireland compared to other
    issues, and why might this be so?
3   How does the treatment of a 'news item' vary over time and what
    factors are likely to influence this?
4   How does the treatment of Northern Ireland in general or a
    specific item on it vary within the media?
5   What do the media focus on: incidents (e.g. murders and
    bombings), events (e.g. elections), policies, trends, or explan-
    ations?

Opposite a number of more specific questions are also raised which
could form the basis of a case study of the media's treatment of Northern
Ireland by focusing on a particular news or current affairs item.

The aim of this approach is almost exclusively process-based with its
emphasis on the skills of critical reading, viewing and listening. Most
issues are constantly moving in and out of public concern while an issue
like Northern Ireland, which stays in the public eye over a long period, is
constantly shifting. Given this turnover of information the media
education approach with its emphasis on transferable skills seems to be a

1 Why has the event been deemed newsworthy? Possibilities here include: it has received 'official' recognition; there was very little else going on; it is sensational; the reporter happened to be in the right place at the right time, etc.

2 Does the presentation favour one view of events? In some ways this question is informed by the subsequent ones, but things to look out for in particular are:

–the use of emotive and rhetorical language;
–the differential status given to different people (e.g. leaving off the title Mr/Mrs/Ms for those seen as outsiders);
–the different styles of interviewing and tone of voice employed with different groups/types of person;
–the amount of time and space given to opposing views.

3 To what extent has the agenda been set by the media for public discussion of the issue by defining the problem in a particular way and deciding what to include and what to omit?

4 How much of the information provided is of a factual nature and how much is opinion? What is the nature of the opinion expressed—expert, informed, partisan, uninformed, etc.?

5 What sources of evidence and information are used? What others might there be?

6 Why have the pictures being used by a particular newspaper been selected to accompany their report? What is the posture and expression of the people photographed? What does the background tell you? What is the relationship between the people? For an example see the questions relating to the photo on p. 24.

7 Why has the film in a TV report on Northern Ireland been selected? What does it tell us? Is there any significance to the particular sequence of shots portrayed, e.g. does the reporter set the scene first or do you see what is happening first? Is the report first-hand or a 'voice-over'?

8 In what ways do the images and the reporting reinforce, contradict or modify each other?

9 Is the issue polarized/dichotomized? (e.g. by such statements as 'Catholics in Northern Ireland view this as' . . .)

10 To what extent are the issues personalized? How justifiable is this? Why might this occur?

11 How might the report be written from a different perspective, e.g. from the point of view of a soldier, a child, a man or woman in the street, etc.?

12 Does the reporter assume that we (the viewers, readers, listeners) share his or her assumptions about what is happening or what needs to be done?

more realistic and more relevant way of dealing with such issues than the straightforward product-based approach of traditional history.

On the other hand, this kind of approach, with its emphasis on 'critical awareness' and an unwillingness to accept public statements at face value from either official or unofficial sources may be controversial in itself. It may also be potentially explosive in politically sensitive areas of the country. Also, as little coverage is given to the background of current events (the media seldom offer a historical perspective), it is unlikely that

ON GUARD: This time it's only a housewife, but in Belfast no soldier takes chances.

1   What do you first notice when you look at this photograph?
2   What message is it trying to convey (e.g. why do you think the 'housewife' is included)?
3   The caption suggests that the 'housewife' is the object of the soldier's attention. Do you agree? What do you think might be happening or going to happen?

pupils will ever wholly unravel the complexities and intricacies of the problems involved. But then with an issue as complex as this it may be that the aim of comprehensive understanding is simply unrealistic.

Empathizing

Whatever the degree of ignorance and the level of emotion that people display concerning the issue of Northern Ireland, there is no doubt that most people in this country cannot understand why or how many people in the Province feel and act as they do. The success of the strike by the Protestant Ulster Workers' Council in April 1974 (direct action by Loyalists against the state), and the election of the Republican, Bobby Sands, as MP for Fermanagh and South Tyrone in 1981 are two examples of events which defied comprehension for most people in Great Britain. For many teachers this failure to appreciate the beliefs and aspirations of the people of the Province provides a block to understanding the issues, while for others the disposition and ability to empathize are worth developing for their own sake as they provide a key with which to understand any issue.

Empathizing is the process of coming to know how another person or group sees the world: what is important to them; what are their beliefs; what are their aspirations; what are their fears/hates/loves; and what considerations they bear in mind when acting and behaving as they do. In order to empathize a person needs first the disposition or the will to see things from another's point of view, and second, the imagination to go beyond the evidence that is available and speculate within a framework different from their usual one. It is important to distinguish empathizing from sympathizing, as one need not believe what another person believed or even feel they are justified or can be excused for their actions in order to know how they feel and why they act as they do.

The extent to which a person needs to have experienced similar feelings and situations and the amount of knowledge that is needed concerning a person or group in order to empathize are questions which remain unresolved. However, it is commonly recognized by teachers that experiential learning and 'listening' to firsthand accounts of the situation are important activities in developing the ability to empathize. Examples of the types of activities that can be undertaken include:

The use of role play
The *Northern Ireland Schools Cultural and Social Studies Project* suggests an exercise which explores the concept of Gerrymandering (**11**). The class is divided into two groups, one larger than the other. The teacher then draws up three 'constituencies' and the smallest of the two groups has a majority in two of them. This is done by having one constituency larger than the others and allocating the majority of the larger group to this constituency. This exercise could then be developed by asking the constituencies to elect two representatives each. The six representatives would then be asked to decide how best to allocate scarce resources (perhaps represented by coloured counters or 'Monopoly' money) between the constituencies. It will not be long before the significance of giving the minority group four representatives compared with the two for the largest group becomes apparent to all. It might also be a good idea after the role play to reverse roles to see how the participants interpret their experiences in the first exercise. This could be followed up by an examination of a map (**12**) of Derry *circa* 1968 showing the distribution of Protestants and Catholics in the three wards. The map clearly demonstrates that the Protestant Unionist vote in total represented 38% of the electorate in Derry in 1968 but that judicious drawing of the

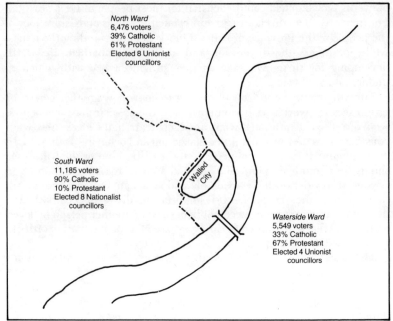

North Ward
6,476 voters
39% Catholic
61% Protestant
Elected 8 Unionist
councillors

South Ward
11,185 voters
90% Catholic
10% Protestant
Elected 8 Nationalist
councillors

Walled City

Waterside Ward
5,549 voters
33% Catholic
67% Protestant
Elected 4 Unionist
councillors

Derry circa 1968

constituency boundaries ensured that the Unionists held two-thirds of the seats in the local Council. The boundaries were re-drawn a year later.

Another interesting approach used by the *Northern Ireland Schools Cultural and Social Studies Project* is a unit about a fictional village called Ballymillis that employs role play and discussion (**13**). The unit comprises an outline of 18 inhabitants of the village and the scenarios of a series of incidents which involve these characters. The aim is to explore the tensions that exist in Ulster without making specific reference to the Troubles. Pupils are supposed to identify with the characters and to seek solutions to the conflicts of values that occur.

While the underlying idea of this unit is useful, there are always potential problems with approaches which create fictional characters as a way of exploring conflict. These stem primarily from the need to simplify the roles in order to highlight certain aspects of the character which will come into prominence during the incidents. The result of this, however, is that the characters are somewhat caricatured. It also seems strange that out of the eighteen central people only two are women!

First-hand accounts
Hearing first-hand accounts of such situations can be an eye-opening experience. One of the most effective lessons that I have seen involved an

ex-soldier who was teaching in another department of the school and was brought in for a history lesson to explain what it was like to be a soldier in Northern Ireland. Having been on two tours of duty he had many graphic accounts of his experience (particularly as a member of the riot snatch squads) and his feelings while there. His growing revulsion at the use of violence and how this had changed him was particularly revealing. While it may not be practical for many teachers to bring in outside speakers with this kind of experience it is possible to obtain a number of accounts of what life is like in Northern Ireland. Two extracts from such accounts are included below. The first is by a Catholic, Eammon McCann, and expresses the kind of frustration felt by a young Catholic at the beginning of the Civil Rights Movement:

> The 1944 Education Act meant that the number of pupils at Catholic grammar schools and of Catholics at Queen's University, Belfast, steadily increased. St. Colomb's in Derry had 725 students on the roll in 1959, 1125 by 1967. For them the contrast between aspiration and local reality was stark. In the early sixties a person like myself could easily get a place at university but would have been ineligible for a job as a lavatory cleaner at Derry Guildhall, and that rankled (**14**).

In the following extract an officer with the Parachute Regiment describes his thoughts while on a routine census patrol:

> I was really quite a nice guy before I came out here. Now I'm looking at this pathetic woman and thinking: swear at me lady and I'll crack you so hard your teeth will fall out. What's happened to me? Belfast, that's what. The city breathes its own cancer and we are right in the middle of it. Build an outer casing around your emotions, enjoy the sense of power, revel in the excitement and the chase, the aggro, the gun battles. Enjoy it. Enjoy it (**15**).

Summary

Without spending a considerable amount of time on this topic there is little hope of developing a full understanding of it. In fact, it may be the case that more harm than good is done; it may lead pupils to feel that they have 'done' Northern Ireland and in this respect a little knowledge may be worse than ignorance. The most realistic way of dealing with this issue in a short period of time would be some form of media analysis along the lines suggested above to encourage pupils to question the assumptions and reasoning behind the presentation of the event as news. On the other hand there seems to me to be a good case for devoting at least half a term within 4th- and 5th-year social studies or humanities programmes to a consideration of this issue in depth.

3

Teaching for unemployment?

Robert Stradling

Less than a decade ago the question 'Should we be preparing young people for unemployment?', would have been inconceivable to most members of the teaching profession. Perhaps the prospect continues to be unpalatable for many teachers but it is no longer unthinkable. The rate of increase in unemployment in recent years has been dramatic. One million unemployed in 1975; two million by August 1980. By the beginning of 1983 there were over three million people on the official register of the unemployed. This meant that about one in eight of the workforce had no job. Just over 40 per cent were in the 16–24 age group and of these 123,807 were school leavers; that is, one in every four young people leaving school could not find employment.

Faced with this situation, teachers — particularly those responsible for careers education — find themselves in an invidious position. Should they be positive, boost morale, encourage appropriate attitudes to work, impart the knowledge and foster the skills necessary for making occupational choices, seeking, obtaining and retaining jobs regardless of the state of the job market? Or, should they prepare school leavers for what may prove to be a long gap between school and work with the prospect of recurrent periods of unemployment throughout their working lives? Of course these two positions are not mutually exclusive and some schools and FE colleges already incorporate both sets of objectives within their vocational education programmes. However, in my experience the former approach still predominates in schools. Many teachers would agree with one headmaster who states, 'I hope we shall never *educate for unemployment*, which is a contradiction in terms and the sort of defeatist realism we can do without' (**1**).

Education for unemployment, then, continues to be a controversial issue for schools. This is not only because it arouses hostility within the profession; nor is it just because it is a significant departure from conventional practice in careers education. Even amongst its advocates it raises controversial questions regarding both the dangers of labelling a group of students within the school or FE college as 'unemployable' (after having already labelled them as 'educational failures') and also the risks of conditioning these particular students into accepting unemployment as inevitable.

In the first half of this chapter, therefore, I shall concentrate on the educational implications of preparing young people for the prospect of immediate and recurrent unemployment and look at how some schools and educationalists approach these problems. In the second part of the chapter I shall go on to consider how teachers might approach the issue of unemployment as a topic within social studies, geography, careers education or social education. In other words, the focus will shift from teaching *for* unemployment to teaching *about* it.

Preparation for unemployment

The school's curricular response to widespread youth unemployment will obviously reflect local circumstances. Undoubtedly it will also reflect certain assumptions — sometimes explicit, frequently implicit and unquestioned — about the nature and causes of unemployment. Essentially there are four competing explanations of the current levels of youth unemployment:

Deficit unemployment — which assumes that school leavers fail to obtain employment because they lack certain basic skills and capacities (e.g. literacy, numeracy and social skills) which employers are looking for.

Voluntary unemployment — which associates youth unemployment with the tendency of the less able young people between the ages of 16 and 20 to gravitate towards seasonal and casual work in the construction and distributive trades or to change jobs frequently as they become bored and dissatisfied with them. This type of unemployment therefore tends to be relatively short-term but recurrent.

Cyclical unemployment — which increases when the economic cycle goes into recession and will decrease when the economy up-turns. In recession young people tend to constitute an unusually high proportion of the unemployed and of this group a high proportion will be school leavers, especially those with low educational attainments. No new jobs are being created, retired workers are not being replaced and few people voluntarily quit. The school leaver is therefore faced with the choice of leaving school, competing for fewer and fewer jobs with people who already have work experience, or remaining in education until the economy recovers.

Structural unemployment — this type of job loss can occur in an industry for a number of reasons. Some industries, like cotton and textiles, have been in a state of decline since the 1950s and that decline is likely to continue. Other industries have shifted gradually and sometimes rapidly from being labour-intensive to capital-intensive. They have done this by **i**) reorganizing the existing production processes to increase productivity (e.g. reductions in overmanning, changes in

existing work practices, introduction of labour-saving practices, etc.)
or **ii**) by partial or total closure of some factories within the industry
(commonly referred to as 'rationalization') or **iii**) by technological
innovation which completely changes the established production
process (e.g. automation and semi-automated production lines).

To some extent, each of these different kinds of youth unemployment
requires a different response from the educational sector. Or, to be more
accurate, when those in authority have assumed that youth unemployment has been due primarily to one of these factors, then they have called
on schools and FE colleges to respond in certain ways. The *Figure* opposite
illustrates the kinds of responses which policy makers have called for.

In the mid-1970s it was widely assumed that youth unemployment was
mainly due to the personal inadequacies of less able school leavers. The
'Great Debate' initiated by the Labour Government in 1976 offered
politicians, employers and even some leading trade unionists the
opportunity to blame schools for rising youth unemployment and, in
particular, to criticize progressive trends in education. The 'back to
basics' movement became more vocal and calls were made for significant
changes in teaching methods and classroom climate. A document issued
by the Manpower Services Commission at the time illustrates their
argument:

> In recent years the social environment in a number of schools, with
> more emphasis on personal development and less on formal instruc-
> tion, has been diverging from that still encountered in most work
> situations, where the need to achieve results in conformity with
> defined standards and to do so within fixed time limits calls for
> different patterns of behaviour. The contrast is more marked where
> changes in industrial processes have reduced the scope for individual
> action and initiative (**2**).

However, by the late 1970s it was becoming increasingly apparent that
in some areas of the country young people leaving school with good
qualifications were also failing to get jobs and in other areas they were
having to lower their expectations and settle for jobs which their counter-
parts leaving school five years before would not have considered. By 1980
the recession was biting deep with 21 registered unemployed for every
notified job vacancy; headlines such as 'Jobs going at the rate of 3000 a
day' and 'Two jobs lost every minute' in *The Guardian* and *The Times*
greeted the announcement of the unemployment statistics in November
1980.

In this situation it was recognized that young people were particularly
vulnerable to cyclical unemployment. School leavers and young people
already in the ranks of the long-term unemployed were likely to be at a
disadvantage when applying for vacancies in competition with redundant
but experienced workers. To some extent the MSC had recognized this in

Educational responses to youth unemployment

Types of youth unemployment	Response from the educational sector
Deficit unemployment Due to lack of the skills and capacities needed by employers	Back to basics Resources directed to remedial education Vocational preparation programmes in FE
Voluntary unemployment Due to lack of commitment to getting and/or retaining a job or to unrealistic expectations	Emphasis on careers guidance and occupational selection Adjusting the curriculum particularly for the less able to better fit the needs of local industry (e.g. Understanding Industry projects, work experience programmes, etc.) General emphasis throughout the formal and hidden curricula on commitment to the work ethic
Cyclical unemployment Due to economic recession	Introduction of short work-experience programmes into careers education New Vocational Preparation courses in FE and final-year school curricula (e.g. City & Guilds Foundation courses) Emphasis on *realistic* job choices, self discipline and work ethic Emphasis for more able on further and continuing education
Structural unemployment Due to economic decline in some industries, structural reorganization in others, and a shift from labour-intensive to capital-intensive production	Emphasis in secondary and FE on producing a more flexible and adaptable workforce Emphasis on further, continuing and recurrent education for all Developing survival skills for coping with extended and recurring unemployment Emphasis on a realistic appraisal of the local job market Introducing into the common core curriculum in schools courses concerned with the broader preparation for adult life (e.g. with titles such as Social Education, Design for Living, Life and Leisure, Social and Life Skills)

1976 when it initiated its *Work Experience Programme* for the young unemployed. By 1978 even more resources were devoted to the *Youth Opportunities Programme* which also aimed to give young people some experience of work and to sharpen school leavers' competitive edge in a declining job market.

Gradually this response has filtered down through the educational system and a growing number of schools have initiated the kinds of responses to cyclical unemployment outlined in the chart.

At present it is clear that policy makers believe that youth unemployment is a temporary phenomenon which will steadily decline as the economic situation improves. Even the MSC's *New Training Initiative* introduced in the summer of 1983 is interpreted as a temporary ameliorative measure. And yet there are growing signs that unemployment in general, and particularly in the more traditional industrial regions of the country, is essentially structural in nature.

During the last ten years the total number of jobs in the economy has remained stable. By the late 1970s the number of people in employment was roughly the same as in the mid-1960s. However, during the last decade the number of people *seeking* work has increased considerably. More women, especially married women, have been joining the job market and the progeny of the 'baby boom' in the '60s has come through the educational system. An economy with a constant number of jobs but a growing labour force generates mass structural unemployment.

To some extent this structural unemployment has been camouflaged by major changes in the patterns of employment. During the 1970s increasing foreign competition and the resulting loss of markets coupled with technological advances in manufacturing meant that over a million jobs were lost in the private sector. But this loss was masked by a growth of over a million jobs in the public sector. Once successive governments embarked on public expenditure cuts to combat a rising rate of inflation, unemployment in the public sector rose rapidly and at the same time highlighted the extent of structural unemployment in the private sector.

Young people have been and still are particularly affected by structural unemployment. The chart below shows the types of employment which many young people traditionally enter on leaving school.

Sources of first-time employment of young people, 1976

	%
Manufacturing	35
Distribution, transport and communication	25
Miscellaneous service industries	12
Professional and financial services	12
Construction	10
Other	6

Source: Holland Report, *Young People and Work*, MSC, London 1977

A large proportion of male school leavers have tended to go into distribution, transport, communications and construction industries. A large proportion of female school leavers have tended to go into the manufacturing sector. It is precisely these areas of employment which have been most severely hit by structural unemployment. Many of these jobs have been permanently removed from the economy so that even if there is an up-turn in the near future there is likely to be persistent unemployment amongst the unskilled young and a contracting market for skilled labour.

In these circumstances an emphasis on the work ethic, remedial education, a 'back to basics' approach, careers guidance or short periods of work experience may improve the competitiveness of some young people but will not significantly improve the situation of the less able. It may also be the case that much of the expenditure by the MSC has also been misconceived and misguided. So, for example, an evaluation of the provision of youth opportunities programmes in the West Midlands, commissioned by the Further Education Unit at the Department of Education and Science, noted that FE lecturers working in areas where youth unemployment was basically structural were rejecting the assumption underpinning the MSC's approach to youth training. Instead they were placing greater emphasis on self-directed learning and the development of 'survival skills' to equip young people not only to look for and retain employment if opportunities arise, but also to use their initiative and take decisions on what to do if no opportunities are forthcoming (**3**).

A further consequence of these processes of structural and technological change is that even those young people who do obtain employment on leaving school are unlikely to experience the sort of stable career patterns which previous generations have known. That is, they may well have to change jobs several times during their working life with intermittent periods of unemployment, and they may need to be periodically retrained and learn entirely new skills. Some educators have recognized this and hence the emphasis in the chart on p. 31 on curricula in secondary and further education aimed at producing a more flexible and adaptable workforce. The kinds of demands likely to be placed on young people in the future are highlighted by Hopson and Scally, in the quotation overleaf reproduced from *Lifeskills Teaching* (**4**).

In vocational training this may well mean a shift away from training to perform specific job tasks towards what the National Economic Development Office calls 'general mechanical intelligence', that is, skills which have a general rather than a specific applicability (**5**). This trend is increasingly apparent in both Technician and Business Education and also in the steady decline in craft apprenticeships.

The demands on secondary education are likely to emphasize the acquisition of attitudes and predispositions in order to help people to cope intellectually and psychologically with recurring changes of job

Someone leaving school today in the UK can expect:

1   three or four different occupations in his or her lifetime;
2   six to ten changes of jobs;
3   to move away from the area of the country he or she was born in;
4   to have probably two marriages;
5   to be involved in education throughout his or her lifetime at different points;
6   to spend some time unemployed;
7   to have a variety of job patterns.

All economic projections indicate the need for a better-educated if smaller labour force. For people without qualifications it is likely to be harder than ever to get jobs that are going.

definition, retraining and periodic redundancy. Demands on education are also likely increasingly to emphasize the need for developing prerequisite skills. To quote Hopson and Scally again:

> With shorter working weeks, flexitime, shift work, job sharing and autonomous job teams making their own production decisions, people will need a higher level of communication, decision making, problem solving and coping skills than ever before (**4**).

Educational implications of structural unemployment

If the above analysis of unemployment is correct, then it is likely that traditional careers education — which appears in one form or another on the curriculum of at least 70 per cent of secondary schools (**6**) — is unlikely to prove a panacea for youth unemployment. Employability skills are undoubtedly useful but as Tony Watts points out:

> It is, however, important to recognize that the advantages such skills offer are essentially relative rather than absolute: their effects are not by and large to increase the number of jobs, but rather to influence the way in which the jobs that exist are distributed. Thus, if all schools focus heavily on the development of these skills, the advantages potentially offered by such a programme may, to some extent, be cancelled out (**1**).

Traditional careers education with its focus on job finding and keeping needs to be supplemented to take account of current employment patterns and trends and this means preparation for future unemployment as well as employment.

Furthermore, structural unemployment tends to be localized. In some parts of the country current unemployment may be mainly due to cyclical factors. In other parts of the country it is likely that job loss will be permanent in those industries which have hitherto been the major employers. Therefore careers teachers, in making decisions about curriculum content, are going to have to do some preliminary research into not only the current job market, but also into likely trends in future employment patterns in their locality. This implies a much closer working relationship with local firms and employers as well as with job centres and careers officers. Statistics on local employment patterns and trends can also be obtained from the statistics division of the Department of Employment (**7**).

The wider curriculum

Provision for preparation for unemployment should be made within the common core for 14–16 year-olds. This would acknowledge the fact that virtually all school leavers — and not just the less able — are likely to experience some periods of unemployment during their working lives. There is also scope for this kind of provision in a number of areas of the curriculum. Subjects such as social studies and community studies — in so far as they focus on the locality and the region – offer opportunities for examining employment patterns, the effect of technological change and Government policies on local industry, and the effects of unemployment on different groups within the community. Traditionally geography teachers have tended to focus on the location of industry, often through local case studies, but perhaps now some consideration should also be given to the geography of job losses (**8**). Social education programmes, or their equivalent, also have a significant contribution to make through their focus on the development of social, communication and survival skills necessary for coping with adult life and through helping pupils to learn how to obtain practical knowledge about their rights and entitlements.

It is important, however, that some attempt is made to coordinate this provision. It is not uncommon to find in schools that the staff in the careers education department do not liaise with staff responsible for social education or community studies. As a result there can often be a serious mismatch in aims and course content. I recall, for example, following pupils through two lessons in one school situated in an area of high structural unemployment. In the first lesson pupils were discussing a field trip in community studies where they had visited local industrial estates. In the lesson they were discussing both the effects of technological change (from labour to capital-intensive plant) and the effects of Government and EEC policies on the region. In a subsequent careers lesson with another teacher, pupils were asked to fill in profiles on their personal qualities and attributes and to match these to a list of jobs. This list was clearly based on traditional employment patterns in the locality rather than on an analysis of present patterns or future trends. Pupils were choosing jobs in local firms who at that time were announcing more redundancies. In my experience this is by no means an atypical case.

Hopson and Scally note that few, if any, careers for school leavers require more than six 'O' levels, yet many schools still have large numbers of pupils studying nine or ten subjects; that job applicants are seldom asked about their examination grades as opposed to passes; and that exam success is no longer a sure guarantee of a job in some areas of the country. This raises the issue of whether a better balance needs to be achieved between examined academic studies and non-examined courses concerned with practical skills and knowledge for adult life. There is also a case for thinking in terms of a significant shift away from what was described in Chapter One as the product-based approach to teaching towards a more process-based approach, i.e. towards regarding knowledge as a *means* to developing transferable skills, processes and concepts rather than as an *end* in itself, a fossilized corpus to be buried in the minds of the next generation.

Curricular design problems

Schools which seek to make a genuine curricular response to the task of preparing young people for unemployment— as opposed to the introduction of the topic of unemployment into an existing and already crowded syllabus—are likely to encounter a number of curricular design problems, as shown opposite.

A key question for any school when deciding how it is going to approach the problem of preparing young people for unemployment or employment is how to resolve the inevitable tension between the needs of society, the needs of industry and the needs of the individual. Undoubtedly one of the major reasons why so much money has been poured into youth opportunities programmes and related schemes is because of fear of social unrest, widespread alienation amongst youth, and repetition of the riots in Brixton, St. Paul's and Toxteth. Also, as we have seen here, industry's perceptions of its needs are gradually shifting and are more concerned now with future needs. For many teachers the main concern may well be individual needs. All three positions are based on certain assumptions about the purpose of education, the role and significance of work in our society and its future role in our lives. Such assumptions need to be made explicit and explored before making curricular decisions.

The previous discussion raises a further issue. Focusing on the needs of society, or the needs of industry, or even the needs of the individual can leave students thinking either that unemployment is due to individual inadequacy or that they are wholly at the mercy of economic and political forces within society. Tony Watts has suggested that in this respect careers education can have any of four very different socio-political functions (1). (See p. 39.)

Potential curricular design problems

A The emphasis on skills leads to a radical departure from conventional course design. Skill development requires repeated practice and reinforcement relating to a range of increasingly varied and complex experiences; and time for learners to reflect on their learning experiences. It is unlikely that process skills (whether for employability, adaptability or survival) can be developed merely by recourse to occasional group exercises, role plays or simulations. The whole course needs to be structured around decision-making and problem-solving exercises, small group discussions and role plays interspersed with direct experience in the community and work places.

B It may be necessary to abandon the more conventional group-paced learning where the pace of learners is determined by the average student. The alternative is to opt for individual-paced learning. Some schools which have moved in this direction have also found it necessary to move away from a course design constructed around a sequence of topics or themes. If each individual student is working at a different rate it is difficult to think in terms of, say, completing work on leisure skills by week six, unemployment benefit by week eight and budgeting by week ten. Instead they operate with a Learning Agenda consisting of a checklist of skills and practical knowledge to be acquired by the end of the course and a set of appropriate and related learning exercises.

C Some schools and FE colleges adopting the individual-paced learning approach have drawn up negotiable personal contracts for students. Individual students, in consultation with the tutor, set themselves short-term feasible learning targets, which are reviewed on a regular basis and re-negotiated. This may seem time-consuming but need not be so if regarded as an integral element of each lesson.

D Formal assessment of performance on such courses seems inappropriate but if it were felt necessary then criterion-referenced assessment would seem to have more potential than the more traditional norm-referenced version; i.e., it is more relevant to ask whether each student is more capable than when the course began rather than whether one student is more able than another. But whether one assesses or not, some kind of feedback to learners is essential on skills-based courses since skilled performance requires reflection on past performance and the capacity to adapt to different circumstances. Some kind of personal profile would seem to be appropriate here.

E Finally, this kind of teaching calls for a wide range of teaching methods and learning activities. For illustration see *An approach to developing survival skills* chart.

Clearly, where a teacher is located on the matrix on page 39 will depend on his or her own personal values. For my part I would locate myself at the interface between the social-change approach and the non-directive approach. The former would entail developing the student's

An approach to developing survival skills

Content development: Survival Skills	Teaching strategy and methods	Teaching materials	Potential constraints
Finding out about rights and entitlements	**Strategy** Skill development requires: –repetition/reinforcement –increasingly varied and complex experiences –time for reflection –feedback to learner on progress	*The Survival Game* –a simulation of coping with Employment Agencies (CSV)	Inflexible time-tabling
Finding out about support services in the community			Prevailing teaching methods in school
Skill in dealing with public officials		*No Bed, No Job* –a board game (CSV)	Pupils' expectations of what school is for
Skill in dealing with employers	*Therefore* –learning needs to be structured to increase gradually the demands on pupils	*Rights Game Kit* –by Small Heath Community Law Centre	Lack of academic status
Skill in living on a limited budget		*Exercises in Personal and Careers Devt.* –nine decision-making exercises by B. Hopson and P. Hough (CRAC, 1973)	Difficult to evaluate its effect
Coping with the kinds of social pressures that the unemployed encounter	–The role of the teacher becomes less directive as students become more skilled		Conventional class-room settings
Coping with psychological effects of not getting a job			
Skill in managing leisure time	**Methods** –Case studies of people who cope successfully or not in different situations	*Deciding* –decision-making exercises, by A. Watts and D. Elsom (CRAC, 1974)	
Solving personal problems	–Simulations and role play –Modelling, coaching of skills		
Making effective personal decisions	–Critical incidents (group thinks each incident through and suggests alternative outcomes)	*Social Skills and Personal Problem Solving* –a range of teaching activities including problem-solving exercises, by P. Priestley et al. (Tavistock, 1978)	
Making and maintaining personal relationships	–Problem-solving exercises –Decision-making exercises		

Four alternative curricular aims relating to unemployment

Social-change approach To help students to see unemployment as a social phenomenon which can only be resolved by political and social change	Individual-change approach To maximize students' chances of finding meaningful employment
Social-control approach To reinforce students' motivation to seek work, and to make them feel that unemployment is a result of personal inadequacy	Non-directive approach To make students aware of the possibility of unemployment, and to help them to determine how they might cope with it and use it positively

awareness of the effects of technological change, the effects of economic and political policies, alternative concepts of work, consideration of criteria for job satisfaction, and awareness of possible economic and political solutions to unemployment and their likely effects on society or certain disadvantaged groups within society. The latter approach would focus on survival and leisure skills.

Teaching about unemployment

In Chapter One a controversial issue was defined as one which 'divides society and for which significant groups within society offer conflicting explanations and solutions based on alternative values'. By this criterion unemployment is undoubtedly controversial. Socially it is potentially divisive. It falls heavily on certain groups in society, particularly those who are already disadvantaged in other ways, such as the low paid, the disabled, school leavers and ethnic minorities. It has also hit certain regions of the United Kingdom such as Northern Ireland, the North East and Wales more heavily than others. On the political scene the parties, the CBI, the TUC and pressure groups such as the Child Poverty Action Group not only advocate different remedies based on different assumptions about the causes of unemployment, they even dispute the extent and effects of it.

Some of the kinds of issues related to unemployment which could be taken up in social studies, humanities and social education lessons are set out in the topic web on the following page. The web includes issues and aspects of unemployment which could be used either as entry points or as subjects for study in depth.

As a topic, 'unemployment' does not lend itself as readily to classroom discussion as other issues. Issues which are essentially disputes over political goals (e.g. self-help versus an extension of the welfare state),

Topic web

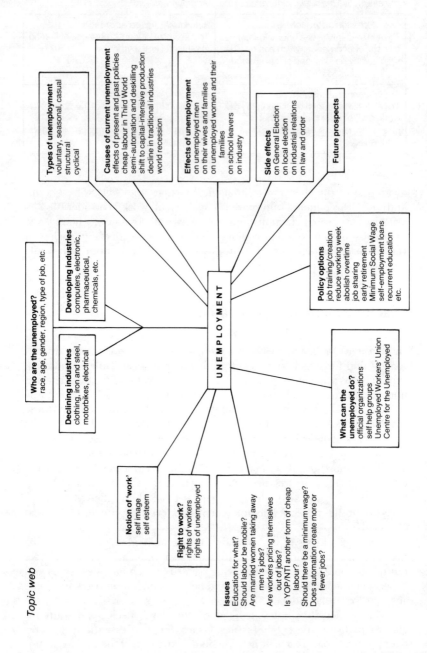

Types of unemployment
voluntary, seasonal, casual
structural
cyclical

Causes of current unemployment
effects of present and past policies
cheap labour in Third World
semi-automation and deskilling
shift to capital-intensive production
decline in traditional industries
world recession

Effects of unemployment
on unemployed men
on their wives and families
on unemployed women and their
    families
on school leavers
on industry

Side effects
on General Election
on local election
on industrial relations
on law and order

Future prospects

Who are the unemployed?
race, age, gender, region, type of job, etc.

Developing industries
computers, electronic,
pharmaceutical,
chemicals, etc.

Declining industries
clothing, iron and steel,
motorbikes, electrical

UNEMPLOYMENT

Policy options
job training/creation
reduce working week
abolish overtime
job sharing
early retirement
Minimum Social Wage
self-employment loans
recurrent education
etc.

**What can the
unemployed do?**
official organizations
self help groups
Unemployed Workers' Union
Centre for the Unemployed

Notion of 'work'
self image
self esteem

Right to work?
rights of workers
rights of unemployed

Issues
Education for what?
Should labour be mobile?
Are married women taking away
    men's jobs?
Are workers pricing themselves
    out of jobs?
Is YOP/NTI another form of cheap
    labour?
Should there be a minimum wage?
Does automation create more or
    fewer jobs?

or moral questions (e.g. abortion), or issues which can be reduced to simple either-or positions (e.g. capital punishment), tend to be well suited to discussion methods. Most pupils will have an opinion and some knowledge, and there is a good chance that alternative points of view will be adequately expressed. But unemployment is a highly complex and multi-faceted issue and unless students already have considerable background information, classroom discussion tends to be sterile.

Some form of enquiry-based project is more likely to prove fruitful; particularly if it is oriented towards unemployment and employment in the local community. There are three potential advantages to this approach:

1 It will give students a better appreciation of not just the personal but also the social implications of unemployment.
2 Students will have an opportunity to acquire relevant firsthand information about local job markets, future employment patterns, their rights and entitlements when leaving school, etc.
3 They will be exercising skills which will be of practical use to them when they leave school and start looking for work or dealing with the Social Security and Unemployment Benefit Offices (e.g. finding out what information they need, distinguishing between useful and irrelevant information, knowing the right questions to ask).

In addition to exercising enquiry skills the project should also encourage students to develop their critical faculties. A spirit of healthy scepticism needs to be cultivated regarding controversial issues, and unemployment is no exception. The public is subjected to a great deal of rhetoric from all sides and representatives of various vested interests use the mass media to present suppositions and propaganda as if they were matters of fact. So in addition to conventional enquiry skills students need to learn how to:

1 ask relevant and probing questions;
2 be able to cope with conflicting evidence and information;
3 evaluate the likely biases of people supplying information and making public statements;
4 make reasonable guesses about whose interests are served by a particular piece of biased information or point of view;
5 plausibly impute motives to the different groups disputing the issue;
6 challenge people's assumptions and preconceptions about unemployment and the unemployed;
7 be critically aware of their own assumptions and preconceptions about the unemployed.

In other words, the project should not be regarded by teachers and students as a mere fact-gathering exercise. It should be seen by all concerned as an opportunity to exercise social and communication skills, the enquiry skills of observation, seeking out, evaluating and using information, and critical thinking skills. These are skills which will have some relevance to everyday life and have the quality of *transferability*. That is to say, they are applicable to other contexts and other issues. Ultimately the 'proof of the pudding' with this sort of approach is that students learn how to ask relevant and searching questions. They may not always obtain satisfactory answers but that is a secondary consideration and tells students more about the nature of bureaucracy than about their own shortcomings.

What is proposed here is that students in 4th- and 5th-year courses (and in pre-employment courses in FE) should work together to construct a *Local Employment Profile* (LEP). Some schools already do work on community profiles, ecological profiles and topographical profiles. A few have begun to profile local employment and unemployment patterns.

The LEP can be done in several ways. Some schools have suspended the 4th-year timetable for a week and involved teachers from a wide range of departments in supervising the work; others have linked social studies and careers lessons for about one month; and yet other schools have devoted six to ten weeks within the common core social studies timetable.

Much, possibly all, of the profiling could be done within the confines of the classroom. But there is a strong case for involving all students in some fieldwork both in their own time and during normal school hours. This will give them experience and confidence in going into Job Centres, Social Security Offices, and employer's premises to seek information, deal with officials and use other forms of communication such as telephones to obtain information.

The Local Employment Profile

Entry points
The introduction to the LEP needs to be carefully thought out. Two different approaches which seem to work are:

i) To explore the group's own knowledge and ignorance of unemployment. This should raise some questions for discussion and future enquiry. Answers to the sample questionnaire in the box below can be checked against the Department of Employment *Gazette* which should be available in the local library reference section.

ii) To discuss how they feel when adults ask them, 'What are you going to be?' Do they assume that these people mean 'What job are you going to do?' Do the students themselves define people in terms of their jobs? In

Questionnaire
1 Roughly how many unemployed people are there in the UK?

1m   2m   3m   4m   5m   6m

2 Which age group is most affected by unemployment?

16–18	30–39
19–20	40–49
20–29	50+

3 Which job category has the highest level of unemployed people?

Shop Assistants	Bus Drivers
Building Labourers	Office Workers
Plumbers	Coal Miners
Postmen	Farm Labourers
Electricians	Car Workers

4 Which region of the country is worst hit by unemployment?
5 Are women more likely to be unemployed than men?
6 Are black workers more likely to be unemployed than whites?
7 How many people in this town are unemployed?

---

what other ways are young people labelled—by teachers, parents and the mass media? What images of young people do the mass media offer? What models do they portray? How do we label the unemployed? What do people mean by 'work'? Is it the same thing as 'having a job'? Is work the main source of our self-image and self-esteem? What is a career? Must a career progress 'upward' or can it progress 'sideways'? This discussion will have raised a whole series of issues to be followed up in subsequent lessons and through a range of enquiries.

Current employment patterns
Which kinds of jobs offer the best and least hope for employment? Who are the unemployed? There are a number of sources of information for questions like these. Each area Job Centre sends information on job patterns (redundancies, vacancies and the unemployed by type of job) to the Statistics Division of the Department of Employment and it is possible to obtain this information about your own area directly from them. The information comes in the form of a computer print-out with a brief code book to interpret it. One possibility therefore might be to work with a teacher responsible for computer studies to devise a simple programme which students could use to find out about local employment patterns. The data could also be up-dated regularly. This might 'kill three birds with one stone': provide background information about the community, provide useful up-to-date information about vacancies for school leavers,

and enable students to become familiar with the school computer in a highly practical way.

In my experience local Job Centres can also be very helpful here. Five centres in the South East, when asked if they would assist students who were conducting an LEP, all readily agreed provided they were not inundated with students, the interview did not last more than one hour, and the visit was on a Friday afternoon (which tends to be the Job Centre's quietest time). Similarly, local careers officers also tend to be very co-operative with projects of this kind.

Future employment and unemployment trends

Here the emphasis is on finding out the main causes of local unemploy-ment and predicting future job changes. Local circumstances can also be compared with national trends. A useful source of information to tap will be the local newspapers and radio stations. Students will have to learn how to interpret news stories about local employers and, above all, how to 'read between the lines'. For example, is the firm announcing redund-ancies solely because it has been hit by the recession or is it shifting from labour- to capital-intensive production. It is by no means always the case but media phrases such as 'temporarily laying-off men', 'going over to a three-day week' and 'cutting back on production' usually indicate cyclical unemployment. Complaints about cheap imports 'flooding the market', demands for state aid or 'more state aid', and references to the 'uncom-petitiveness of the home industry' are usually early signs of an industry going into decline. References to 'overmanning', 'streamlining the workforce', 'robots on the shop floor' usually foreshadow structural unemployment (**9**).

In addition, the interviews with staff at job centres and careers offices might also be used to find out what they think are the likely trends in future unemployment. Do they anticipate more structural unemployment and in which firms? Do they see any signs of economic recovery?

Visits to local firms or visits to school from personnel officers of local firms give pupils an opportunity to ask about future trends, e.g. is the firm considering cutting back production? Are they introducing new labour-saving production techniques?, etc.

Social effects of unemployment

The experiences of being out of work, searching for work, living below the poverty line: this topic is often fraught with problems for the teacher. Very little is known about the effects of unemployment on women—the focus has almost always been on men. The dividing line between a useful avenue of enquiry and a serious invasion of privacy is a thin one. Clearly in most classrooms now there will be young people with direct experience of unemployment within their families but they may not wish to talk about it. Similarly it is difficult to predict how people-in-the-street will react to being asked about life on the dole. On one field trip I observed, children from a school in a middle-class catchment area visiting an inner-city area of high unemployment generated considerable ill feeling leading to muttered comments such as 'Come to see the animals in the zoo, have you?' But this is not always a problem.

It may therefore be advisable to start by looking at published accounts. *Tell Them From Me* by Gow and McPherson (**10**) draws on letters written by young people a year after leaving school. (See also Allinson and Harrison (**11**) and Pahl (**12**).) Former pupils might also be persuaded to come back and talk about their experiences in the first year after leaving school. Officials in the local social services departments may also be willing to:

i) discuss their policies for dealing with unemployment;
ii) comment on the strain on their current resources;
iii) provide specific information for testing hypotheses, e.g. in an area of relatively low employment the Department may give information about the waiting-lists for council housing, school places, etc., since all this information would be relevant to deciding whether or not it is easy for people to move from one locality to another in search of work.

Other possibilities here include checking out stories about the unemployed which appear in local and national newspapers. If the local press prove uncooperative or the stories cannot be checked, then students can at least decide which questions they would need to ask to test the truth or significance of the story.

The unemployed's rights

There are a number of work packs and simulations on the market which are useful here. The Small Heath Community Law Centre has published the *Rights Game Kit* (**13**) which is a simulation focusing on the kinds of legal problems which the unemployed typically face. The National Youth Bureau has published a guide to the law as it affects young people (**14**) and the National Extension College has a brief handbook entitled *Coping with the System* (**15**).

Staff at Advice Centres and local branches of the Claimants' Union might also be prepared to be interviewed by students and explain the kinds of legal problems workers and unemployed people tend to face.

Help for the unemployed

Information can be collected from the local education authority, the Job Centre and the FE college regarding training, re-training and vocational preparation programmes and other courses for the unemployed.

Another possibility would be to invite a speaker from the local Trades

Council to talk about what, if anything, the local branches of trade unions and the TUC are doing for the unemployed. For example, some Trades Councils, with support from the TUC, have established local branches of the Unemployed Workers' Union, usually based at the Trades Council's offices. The TUC, with help from the MSC and local authorities, have also set up over 130 Centres for the Unemployed (details from the local Job Centre).

Issues within an issue
Once students are becoming more informed about the local situation they should be able to investigate and test a number of statements made by people in authority which are highly controversial. For example:

> *People ought to get on their bikes and look for work.*
> *People can get work in other parts of the country if they are prepared to move.*
> *Married women are taking away men's jobs.*
> *Workers are pricing themselves out of jobs.*
> *Automation creates new jobs.*

Once again, if it is not possible to get sufficient information to test these 'hypotheses', students can at least decide what kinds of questions they would need to ask and what kinds of information they would need to obtain.

Side issues
Clearly side issues would depend on particular local circumstances. For example, does unemployment seem to be an issue at the local council elections? Are local employers blaming schools and FE colleges, or the recession, or 'unfair foreign competition'? Does high unemployment have implications for other controversial issues such as industrial relations? The press cuttings opposite, for example, offer some scope for discussion of this particular side issue.

What can the unemployed do?
Here, too, it is likely that activities will vary from town to town. In Merseyside, for example, unemployed people have set up a Skills Exchange Project (Rally Merseyside) in which they can exchange their services (e.g. a plumber and a motor mechanic) in a form of barter. Other self-help groups are being set up in rural areas, small towns and inner city areas. There may also be community projects in your area staffed by the unemployed. Students can obtain background information through, for example, the *Don't let them waste your time* pack available from Community Service Volunteers (**16**). The local community could then be compared with other communities.

Mr John Biffen, Trade Secretary, yesterday urged fainthearted colleagues in the Conservative Party to look on the bright side of the present economic crisis. Though harsh in terms of short-term personal misery, he said, high unemployment had brought some significant advantages to the country as a whole.

... he went on to list four areas of the domestic economy in which the consequences of high unemployment had been welcome. They included a reduction in over-manning, a sharp fall in the number of strikes, a lower level of pay settlements, and the halving of the rate of inflation from its peak of just over 22 per cent.

The Guardian, 11 August 1981

Fear of unemployment—and the recession—have had their effect on the much-publicized militancy of the Coventry car workers. Talbot, like several companies, has been emboldened to press ahead with new manning levels and work practices at its Ryton assembly plant in spite of union opposition. 'Two years ago such a move would have been unthinkable. Now the workers know it would be foolish to pick a fight. With so much unemployment, the company holds all the cards', says one senior shop steward.

Financial Times, 28 January 1981

Policies for unemployment

It is probably advisable to leave this topic until last. By then students will have acquired enough information to look at policies critically and constructively. Brainstorming sessions in small groups should produce a range of policies and not just the more conventional and officially sanctioned ones. Possible policies include:

> Government-funded job training and job creation schemes
> reducing the working week
> abolishing overtime
> job sharing
> early retirement
> part-time employment
> recurrent education
> freelancing and moonlighting
> Minimum Social Wage
> self-employment loans and grants

Local Employment Profiles need considerable planning and discussion amongst the staff before they are attempted. They will tend to be more effective if the skills they involve are developed and exercised throughout the social studies or social education programmes and not just in the project work. It is also possible that as a result of these enquiries students will come up with proposals for action. This of course can be a potential hot potato and because of this it is advisable to involve senior staff in the school in the initial planning phase and to ensure that this possibility is discussed and decided on in advance.

4

Sexism and the curriculum

Bridget Baines

The Equal Opportunities Act of 1975, by its recognition that many individuals in our society suffer adverse discrimination on the grounds of their sex, helped to bring the public's attention to a debate about a number of related issues. In the educational context issues raised have included: equal access to all aspects of schooling; positive support for girls or boys who want to study subjects not traditionally associated with their sex; socialization into traditional and stereotypical roles; equal treatment of students in the class and of male and female staff; the problems of biased teaching materials and textbooks.

Some clarification of terms may be helpful. 'Sexism' is commonly used to describe prejudice or adverse discrimination on the basis of either a person's sex or stereotypical views of masculine and feminine roles. Key elements of sexism are behaviour, attitudes or actions which urge individuals towards conformity with stereotypes or result in their being labelled as 'different' or 'eccentric' if they do not conform. While sexism always has implications which are adverse to one sex, 'sex-bias' (giving prominence to, or favouring, one sex) is not necessarily adversely discriminatory. For example, by specifically encouraging girls to involve themselves in such activities as craftwork or a computer club you may not be discriminating against boys. 'Male' and 'female' refer to biological differences, but 'masculine' and 'feminine' refer to culturally ascribed attributes (which may vary from one culture to another).

Clearly in many schools the question of what, if anything, should or could be done is a highly contentious one. Controversy centres on the following questions:

i) whether or not sexism exists at all;
ii) whether sex-bias is really undesirable;
iii) what forms it takes;
iv) whether schools have a role in dealing with it.

Consensus on any of these is seldom reached, and discussion amongst the staff in schools can provoke ill-feeling and aggression. This issue cannot be confined to topics, lessons or materials. It involves questions of teaching style and aims, and may therefore be seen by some staff as questioning their 'professionalism'.

Even when an institution takes positive action to reduce sex biases and increase opportunities it may be that changes will be constrained and even nullified by those factors in a school which are now commonly referred to as 'the hidden curriculum'. In this Chapter I shall therefore look at the scope for change in both the planned and the hidden curriculum; the scope for introducing sexism as a topic in the humanities and social studies; and the scope for change in teaching styles and methods in order to reduce sex-biases.

Curriculum planning

The following extract illustrates an anti-sexist policy devised by staff in Clissold Park School. What the teachers there have done is to conduct a three-stage review: a working party looked into all aspects of the problem, their report was considered by a larger group of staff, and a policy was devised for future work which has now actually taken place (1).

ANTI-SEXIST/EQUAL OPPORTUNITIES POLICY AT CLISSOLD PARK SCHOOL, HACKNEY

We view with concern the findings of the anti-sexist working-party report. In particular we note that:

1 Girls in selecting options are reluctant to move beyond traditional female subjects, thus narrowing their potential development.
2 Girls underachieve as a result of their low expectations.
3 There is a disproportionate representation of men in senior positions in the school, particularly in pastoral jobs.
4 There is a lack of formal response by the curriculum at present to the emotional, social and intellectual problems facing girls.
5 There is a passivity amongst the majority of girls making them reluctant to seek teacher attention.

In response, the staff commits itself in principle to:

1 Positive anti-sexist content within the foundation and personal development courses.
2 Departments examining curriculum resources and practice in order to attempt to eliminate sexism.
3 The creation of a post of responsibility for the coordination of anti-sexist policy within the school.
4 An allocation of resources to be made available in order to carry out these proposals.
5 Consideration in the appointment of staff to the balance of sexes in the school, particularly in senior positions.

Other schools have developed policies in slightly different ways but all of them have had to give considerable thought to staff development. The key problems are how best to persuade some members of staff—and these may often include some women as well as male members of staff—a) to evaluate critically their teaching to see if it is biased or perpetuates any disadvantages; b) to examine the scope for change in course content, methods and teaching style. The involvement of advisory staff, teachers' centre leaders and outside speakers can significantly contribute to staff development within the school. The participation of governors and parents and the designation of individual members of staff to coordinate the implementation of the agreed policy will also help to convince everyone of the importance and relevance of the policy and increase the likelihood of success.

Inter-departmental work is also important. It will supplement and support the work carried out in individual departments and be of particular help to those groups of teachers from different disciplines who are currently cooperating on core curriculum courses in the humanities, careers or social education. The experience of schools approaching the issue in this way is that much of the potential controversy may be reduced.

Some schools have found that the timescale involved may be longer than they initially expected. Developing a policy, reviewing materials and even making minor changes to the curriculum can often take from two to five years. It also seems common for there to be a hiatus at around eighteen months, with sagging enthusiasm and uncertainty about future action. Some schools have responded by taking stock of progress, changing the membership of the working group a little, or again bringing in speakers from outside. Producing a report or an article, working on an activity day or display involving pupils may also help—anything that enlivens interest and brings some sort of psychological reward.

Some forms of review necessitate the involvement of departments or large sections of staff, especially such possibilities as

a) breaking down subject barriers, or regrouping to give easier access to subjects previously thought of as discrete;
b) consideration of 'remedial' classes; (Some schools have noted the benefit to both sexes of single-sex groups for this.)
c) review of the option choice arrangements and advice to pupils;
d) consideration of the effects of the hidden curriculum and the dependence of subject teachers on this.

Curriculum content

Teachers concerned with sexist bias in the curriculum tend to focus on three areas:

1) the omission of content about women;
2) the portrayal of their roles as stereotypical, unimportant or irrelevant;
3) the skills and thought processes fostered in pupils, and the ways in which this is done.

Omission of content about women

Some examples may illustrate many of the difficulties. For instance, the use of 'man' in the title of one course has posed some unexpected problems. A teacher who asked her class to illustrate and write about *Man and his Environment* (the title of a first-year course) found to her dismay that most of the boys left women out, while the girls and the remaining boys either portrayed women under 'the environment' or (in a few cases) changed the title to 'Man/Woman'. On trying a similar exercise with another group, using the title *People and their Environment*, there was no such confusion.

Although this is a small example on its own, it echoes a common problem, for while the use of 'he' is meant to imply that women are included, how and where is often unclear in the rest of the course. For instance, women are often completely overlooked in some history courses—relegated to the role of royal wives and mistresses. Roman history focuses almost exclusively on the military and colonial administration, yet not all Romans were soldiers or senators. Were women's activities purely domestic or were there women in other occupations? Writers such as Pliny or Martial might give insights into these and other aspects that would provide a welcome supplement to the prevailing military histories of Julius Caesar and others.

Similar questions can be raised about British history. Wars, for example, have always changed women's occupations and roles. This applies as much to the Crusades as to the First and Second World Wars. Until the early nineteenth century women often played a major role in agriculture and cottage industries. The guilds are often presented in history books as a male preserve, yet there have always been women's guilds and guilds where women formed the majority of the membership, particularly in crafts such as the Haberdashers, the Fishmongers and the Hatters. Female ownership of property and the running of businesses only started to decline during the Victorian era. Indeed, as with other aspects of British history, the preoccupations of Victorian historians influenced their interpretation of their own and previous eras and continue to act as filters for our own perceptions of previous generations.

Often the role of women is also omitted from the study of other societies. Again, consideration could be given to such questions as: What are the occupations of women in predominantly agricultural societies? What happens under circumstances of change, westernization and the introduction of technology? What part do women play (or what role is assigned to them) in the religious beliefs of different groups and how are they affected by them? What rights do women have and which rights will custom permit them to exercise in such societies? Such questions are essential to a genuine understanding of the particular cultures, peoples and times under study.

Where original sources fail to offer information about such roles at a given time or place, contemporary textbook writers can hardly be blamed for omissions. However, there are numerous examples of texts and materials ignoring women when data are readily available: but it is often more difficult to raise questions than to find answers, so accustomed are we to the status quo and conventional perspectives.

Stereotyping

Teaching materials on anything from law and order to trade unions, from medicine to agriculture, often appear to be entirely male-oriented. Similarly, nursing, childcare, factory, domestic and shop work often appear as the sole preserve of females. The assumptions behind such representations are conveyed to pupils and can affect their views of themselves and others. A useful checklist for detecting sex stereotyping in teaching materials can be found in Stinton (**2**) or could be adapted from the one developed by Hicks for detecting racial stereotyping (**3**).

Skills development

Reviewing the sorts of skills and learning processes being fostered in the classroom is a complex task made more so by the range of individual teaching styles in any school. It has been suggested by a number of studies (**4**) that girls may be less likely than boys to speak at any length in front of a large group; less likely to gain the teacher's attention for any length of time; less likely to initiate new ideas; and less likely to use either the space of the classroom or the equipment and resources to their fullest extent. Some teachers, alerted to these possibilities, have tried to vary their teaching methods. Small-group learning, including learning in single-sex groups, enables the less confident boy or girl to have a more positive role. However, several points have to be borne in mind:

- —If all pupils are expected to take a full part in the task or activity, the groups may have to be as small as three or four.
- —With mixed groups, it is still possible for the boys to cut the girls out of the activity, or to give them the same role time after time (such as taking notes). It happens less often the other way round!
- —Even where small groups within the class are single sex it is possible for the boys to continue to dominate the classroom, teachers' time, and also such things as reporting back, display areas or materials.
- —With single-sex groups it is also possible for pupils to opt for particular stereotypical topics if the teacher gives a completely free choice.

Current emphasis on study skills and social and life skills is leading to greater use of enquiry-based and genuinely student-centred learning. Yet there is some evidence that teachers make too few demands of girls and give them less encouragement, support and time than the more socially dominant boys. Thus a self-perpetuating cycle of inhibition, inactivity and low confidence can develop.

In large groups, or with the whole class, care needs to be taken to ensure that the content, materials, and activities are not dominated by the boys. Questioning a whole class and expecting individual pupils to volunteer answers may not be an appropriate way of developing skills. Where teachers reverse this process and make the pupils ask them questions, two things are noticeable: the quality of questions tends to be higher, covering more of the topic; and larger numbers of pupils, especially girls, take part. This method seems also to foster language skills.

Many teachers using these and other methods and encouraging the development of these skills have noted an improvement in both sexes, particularly in confidence and cooperation with members of the peer-group (1). It may be that such features are as much a case of 'good teaching' as avoiding sexism.

The hidden curriculum

So much has now been said and written about the hidden curriculum that it cannot be ignored. Clearly there are more ways of communicating information, especially about values, attitudes and assumptions, than by stating them outright—even, that it is possible to state one thing and strongly indicate the reverse through the structures and daily arrangements of the school. As the introduction to the discussion document *Equal Choices for Girls in the Secondary Curriculum*, drawn up by Devon LEA, notes:

> Even when a school has managed to make all parts of the subject curriculum equally accessible to both sexes—and even that problem appears not to have been overcome in some schools—it still has to ensure that at least some of the influences which act against equality of opportunity can be cancelled out.

The hidden curriculum involves many such 'influences' which convey to pupils a whole range of unquestioned attitudes, values and assumptions through social aspects of school life such as the following:

- –institutional organization
- –classroom organization
- –interaction in and out of the classroom, including behaviour encouraged or discouraged, and the preconceptions and assumptions of teachers and students.

Institutional organization

The deployment of staff conveys messages to the pupils. Thus, with a mixed staff, if most of the senior posts are held by men, children may lack positive role models of 'able' and 'successful' women and have some of their stereotypes of men and women apparently endorsed and therefore strengthened. For instance, in 1976 31.2% of all male teachers were on scale 4 or above, compared with only 13.2% of women teachers (**5**). One headteacher put it like this:

> A lot of this comes down to staff-training. It's not enough to say 'we want more women in senior posts'. Most heads 'groom' teachers for posts—give them practice with timetabling, for instance. Heads of large schools tend to be men and they're more likely to feel easy working with the male staff. Sometimes it just doesn't occur to them that the women really want the responsibilities, even when the evidence is there. So the women may not be encouraged to get the experience.

The subjects that male and female teachers are associated with (males with science, metalwork, technical drawing; females with English, home economics and office studies) also convey information which may influence pupils' choice regardless of their aptitude. Breaking with convention, say by employing a male home economics teacher or a female teacher of technical drawing, may not necessarily have much immediate impact. One school which employed a female metalwork teacher did not immediately find large numbers of girls opting for the subject. Four years later rather more girls were opting for it than before and were more likely to stay the course. However, genuine change is more likely to occur when subject areas are reorganized into general groupings, such as metalwork becoming part of craft, design and technology.

Classroom organization
The ways in which pupils are grouped for teaching or administrative purposes may increase the possibilities for divisions and sex-bias in mixed schools. Two major studies (**6**) have shown how the use of sex-segregated registers for allocating seating and equipment in science and craft lessons resulted in the same few girls being regularly without equipment, or having to fill in for those who were absent, or having to work in awkward corners. Humanities and arts teachers may be less likely to seat pupils in this way, but many monitor work, arrange small groups for tasks, or allocate materials and duties by register. This can lead to the same few getting the least amount of attention, assistance or quality materials. Some teachers say openly that if there are insufficient books to go round, then they will ask the girls to share, since they tend to behave better in these circumstances than boys.

Where pupils' seating arrangements are permanently segregated into territories (by their choice or the teacher's) so that large areas of the classroom can be designated 'the boys' side' or 'the girls' corner', then their work and their contact with the teacher may be affected. Exchange between pupils or groups may be reduced. The classroom, and the equipment available in various parts of it, may impose limitations if pupils will not go into a particular area because it is seen as 'the territory' of the opposite sex.

Classroom interaction

This refers to all the social communication occurring between pupils and the teacher, or among the pupils themselves. It can include verbal and non-verbal communication, such as eye-contact (for control, support or assistance), or body language (such as towering over a pupil in a threatening way, or sitting down next to a group).

Monitoring of teaching in some schools reveals that many teachers do not give equal attention to girls and boys in their classes, tending to concentrate their efforts chiefly on the boys. The quality of attention, too, can vary. There may be very good reasons for this, related to discipline and classroom management. Teachers need to notice and keep an eye on those likely to misbehave in order to pre-empt them. In mixed classes these are more likely to be boys than girls, and the boys may therefore be the main influence on teachers' behaviour.

Pupils' own assumptions about the attention they should receive can cause them to put extra pressure on a teacher to conform to 'norms', even when she or he is attempting to create a more equitable balance of attention. While many of the girls may show very positive responses, teachers' initial efforts to remedy the situation may also lead some boys to become more demanding socially. Teachers encountering this feel that a gradual change in the atmosphere of the classroom needs to be built up, that trust and respect rather than competition are important.

Pressure on boys to behave in 'acceptable' masculine ways can be as inhibiting as the social pressure on girls, especially where the aesthetic and emotional fields of experience are concerned. The ridicule of a boy or man if he shows appreciation or understanding of music, art or literature (particularly poetry), or if he fails to conceal fear, doubt, tenderness or sorrow, limits his human potential and can increase his difficulties with relationships and his empathy with others. Such pressures may also influence choice of career, as boys wishing to train as nurses, dancers or artists have found. Some boys, like girls, may experience forms of covert sexual harassment.

The changes in school organization and teaching styles which may be necessary if the constraints of the hidden curriculum are to be countered, would seem to raise a dilemma for the teacher. The potential reduction in pupil choice, and the need to pressurize pupils towards activities they might not otherwise wish to engage in, may seem like a denial of some of the tenets of child-centred, liberal education. However, this need not be the case. Teachers involved in efforts to promote equal opportunities often speak in more positive terms of support and encouragement for pupils attempting to be active in curricular areas which might hitherto have been unfamiliar. They are concerned with fostering a wider range of skills and assumptions about roles to try to prevent option and career choices being based as much on the absence of certain skills as on those skills which have been acquired.

Sexism as a topic

Teaching strategies

Most teachers dealing with this issue will have at least a commitment to the line supported by the Equal Opportunities Act and DES policies. Although a number of the teachers working on policy documents and new courses may be feminist or have sympathies with some feminist viewpoints, there are many committed to this work who do not subscribe to any of the feminist ideologies. Many teachers make this distinction clear to pupils and think this is an important point, enabling pupils to judge the views and materials presented. Furthermore, teachers often remember their own gradual move towards their present position, indeed their views may still be undergoing change, and therefore would neither expect nor wish pupils to adopt such views totally, or without question. The issue is a very fluid one, and viewpoints are questioned to a much greater degree even than when dealing with racism.

A few points about the subject of *indoctrination* seem apposite here. Alarm at the possibility of indoctrination arising from the teacher's statement of a point of view or commitment seems to stem from unproven assumptions about the strength of a teacher's influence and the classroom context. To begin with, the teacher here is not in the same position as, say, physics or modern languages teachers, in that she or he is not initiating pupils into a body of knowledge or a set of discipline-related skills. Instead the teacher is intervening in a well-established learning process. Pupils bring with them their own relevant experiences, preconceptions, attitudes and behaviour. They also have some idea of the teacher's opinions or may assume them in this context by the very choice of the issue. In this situation, for the teacher to attempt an apparently neutral stance would be artificial, dishonest and potentially confusing.

In such circumstances indoctrination or conditioning are unlikely to have much effect even if it were thought to be advisable. Also, much of the discussion about indoctrination appears to assume the predominance of teaching as instruction. Where a teacher does not teach in this way his or her view will be invested with much less authority—a point needing to be made perhaps more frequently and strongly. Most of the techniques and teaching methods used for this issue seem to be designed to open up a wider range of views for debate and to allow more space for consideration and response, both private and public. This does not seem to square with the attempt 'to teach something as if it were true or universally acceptable regardless of evidence to the contrary, or in the absence of any evidence at all', a definition of indoctrination referred to in our introduction. In fact one could argue that attempts to avoid facing up to the issue of sexism in both the hidden and planned curriculum may be akin to indoctrination by default.

The view of a woman's place is a social and cultural one, and many teachers work in schools with pupils from diverse ethnic backgrounds. In this situation there will of course be views of women's roles different even from the range found within the traditions of English society. Teachers need to be particularly sensitive to this. There is sufficient controversy within most cultures now about the place of women for these discussions to include more than a mere 'status quo' approach where other cultures are concerned, and teachers working with pupils from diverse ethnic backgrounds need to inform themselves wherever possible about the customs of those groups. In some cases it may help to split classes into single-sex groups to allow greater freedom of speech and diminish the possibility of individuals being upset or feeling threatened.

Teachers in single-sex schools often feel that they have some advantages and some disadvantages over those in co-education. The advantages seem to be that the planned curriculum is often less sharply divided into girls' and boys' subjects, and that some topics relating to sex-bias may be discussed more openly, such as male and female sexuality, sexual harassment or prostitution. The disadvantages lie chiefly in the absence of firsthand views from the opposite sex which could lead to useful exchanges.

In many boys' schools the issue may be seen as totally irrelevant to the pupils, and this creates practical problems for teachers who feel that it does concern them both in terms of their own self-perception and their views of women and girls. Nevertheless, in some boys' schools courses include sexism as a topic or include modules looking at the experiences of women and girls as well as boys and men in family and society, and developing skills such as sewing and cooking. Some teachers attempt to provide time for discussion of masculine and feminine images, and to support less aggressively 'masculine' views and behaviour.

Course strategies

Sexism is not easily containable in a topic or case-study. Pupils' attitudes and experiences may lead them to hold strong views on the subject, and discussions may have implications for, and effects on, life beyond the classroom. In addition, actual knowledge of laws, statistics and case histories relating to equal opportunities will probably be limited, thus diminishing the possibility for reasoned discussion. Therefore, it may be necessary to tackle the issue on several fronts:

     i)   provision of information
    ii)   discussion of possible implications
   iii)   demythologizing
   iv)   clarification and discussion of attitudes.

In the light of these, it may be that a product-based approach to teaching, as described in Chapter One, is inappropriate here. The emphasis on knowledge transmission could exclude the development of skills necessary for the critical evaluation of different viewpoints, including an awareness of one's own assumptions. However, a purely process-based approach could exclude too much of the content on which views and arguments might be more solidly based. A combination of the two seems most suitable. In my experience, when teachers are dealing with this issue there tends to be a gradual shift in teaching style. There is a generally held view that enabling the pupils to air and discuss their views is of paramount importance, and teaching methods are usually chosen which maximize this possibility. Some teachers even choose this issue on the grounds that it engages pupils in forms of debate in which they confront their own bias in a way encouraged by few other topics.

Modular courses

A possible structure for a course focusing on this issue might be:

1   Helping girls and boys to identify their own feelings about sex-bias and equal opportunities.
2   Looking at examples of representation of girls and boys/men and women in the media and literature—magazines, books (including those already in use with the class), television, advertising, art.
3   Considering roles: stereotyping and atypical roles could be included here.
4   Considering language associated with various roles; relationships with other people demonstrated by language forms; vocabulary or sayings associated with one sex or the other. Discussion of possible reasons, motives or concepts underlying such usage.
5   Looking briefly at a number of topics in relation to women's and men's lives, e.g. family, school, the law, local and national government, employment and unemployment.
6   Hypothesizing about causes, effects, possible action if desired.

Discussion of pupils' own and other people's views and attitudes would be important at all stages. It is necessary continually to resist oversimplification, stereotyping and polarization, the latter being a particular risk with this issue as it is easy to fall into a 'girls v. boys' approach. Formal debates or 'for-and-against' arguments may pressurize pupils towards an artificial consensus which could reduce awareness of the complexity of the issue.

It is possible for pupils to be distanced and the issue clouded by too much input of content, or activities which do not seem to be related to the pupils' own experience. This danger may be higher than for many issues because pupils *expect* their experience to be relevant to it in some way or another (while in contrast they are unlikely to have personal experience of issues such as the Third World or nuclear weapons). Introductory work focusing on experiences of family life or peer groups is common.

Here are some examples of teaching notes outlining possible lessons on three topics which open up for discussion attitudes to masculinity and femininity.

A   Games and activities
   i)   Pupils work individually or in small groups, drawing up lists of six games and activities they think might be suitable for boys and six for girls.
   ii)   Discuss in small groups of four or five.
   iii)   Ask for reports from each group and list on blackboard. Leave space to the right of each list to draw in later columns.

Boys	*Girls*
swimming	swimming
football	dancing
car mechanics	sewing
computer games	cooking
canoeing	netball

   iv)   Ask them to discuss and write down games or activities listed as being suitable for one sex but in which they know members of the other sex who take part.
   v)   Asking the groups to report back, add a column to the right of those already on the board, e.g.:

Boys	*Some Girls*
swimming	
football	
car mechanics	

   vi)   Ask groups to discuss a) which activities listed for the other sex they would engage in and why they appeal, and b) which they wouldn't, and why.
   vii)   Brief report back/full class discussion.

Topics which could be treated in a similar way might include housework, male/female characteristics, school subjects, comics, etc. I observed the second of these being used particularly successfully to engender a sensitive and far-reaching discussion with a group of 13–14-year-olds.

B   *Analysis of media images*
  i)   Collect as wide a range of magazines, newspapers and comics as possible (with help from pupils) before lesson.
  ii) Ask small groups (three or four pupils) to cut out three to six pictures of men and women and glue them to two large sheets of paper (per group).
  iii) Groups then discuss and list the following:

    a)   characteristics portrayed for each;
    b)   activities shown or indicated, or omitted;
    c)   jobs suggested by picture or caption;
    d)   the message the picture might be trying to convey, and to whom;
    e)   for what purpose was the picture used (e.g. advertising, illustrating a story/report, etc.);
    f)   do they consider the picture was or would be successful for this purpose?

  iv) Short report back and full class discussion.
  v)   Further questions (either for discussion or writing):

    a)   What differences were there in the portrayal of the two groups?
    b)   What differences were there in the purposes for which they were used?
    c)   Give three examples of pictures where the substitution of someone from the opposite sex would be possible, and three where it would be impossible. Say why in each case.

With a number of small adjustments, such as quantity of questions and types of material looked at, this could be adapted for several types of course or age group. Similar work could stem from the use of film or video.

C   *Language*
  i)   Before the lesson, devise task cards outlining different short situations involving males only, females only, and a mixture. There should be some variety, formal and informal.
  ii) Divide the class into groups of two to five pupils and give each a card. Ask them to prepare a short piece of dialogue based on the situation on their card. (Monitor progress unobtrusively if possible, to help make decisions about later use of their material.)
  iii) Ask groups to act or read their dialogue.

iv) Ask the groups to reverse all the sexes in their dialogue (i.e. male characters become female) without changing the actual script and re-perform some (selections might be best).

v) Discuss why some of the dialogue is odd/funny/inappropriate etc. (or ask pupils to discuss/write in groups).

This work might be preliminary to a range of further work on language, roles, social interaction and expectation, etc., depending on the type of course and length of time available.

Sex-bias and men can also be discussed as a topic. This may include the consideration of disadvantages as well as advantages for men; stereotyping and its effects; society's pressure on men to compete for careers with status, to support families and carry major burdens of responsibility without showing signs of resultant stress; bias in work conditions, and the implications of paternity leave were it to be introduced; role reversal in families (especially under pressure of unemployment and redundancy); homosexuality.

The above would be suitable for modules in social studies/English language/social education and other similar courses (**9**). A module in a history or English literature course might have to be much less inter-disciplinary in style. Some teachers argue that it is no more than 'lip-service' to include a module on, say, women in history, or sex-roles during the Second World War, but that such material should be infused into the whole course. Work which could be adjusted to either approach could include the study of men's and women's occupations or influence in specific periods, places, or in relation to particular events. Home/working life during the early industrial revolution, or enquiry-based studies of occupations in the area of the school during the last two decades of the nineteenth century, or a study of women's and men's activities during the wars (including women at the front and men who remained in Britain, and the consequent changed occupations of both groups), are examples of this. Materials are sometimes difficult to come by, and teachers may have to rely on collating material from several sources (**10**). For instance, some suggestions for a history course from a local history librarian (**7**) include the following:

1 *The London Tradesman* by R. Campbell, 1747 (reprinted 1969, David and Charles). This includes tradeswomen.

2 Indenture papers. These show girls' trades and also women as 'masters'.

3 Household accounts show payments to tradespeople (e.g. 'to Ann Westerband, plumber—£1.7s.0' from accounts of the Duke of Richmond, Greenwich, 1734).

4 *Universal British Directory* for the 18th century.

5 Churchwarden's accounts—payments to women in businesses, etc.

6   Poor Law papers for the examination and settlement of paupers.
7   Census returns.
8   Parish registers. Some included women's occupations, especially during the First World War.
9   Factory journals.
10   Photographs.

Such sources can be tapped by the pupils themselves or made into packs by groups of teachers. An example of the latter is a study of a nineteenth-century silk mill owned by Courtaulds at Halstead in Essex. The teachers and a teachers' centre leader drew upon the research of a PhD student at Essex University, turning some of her material into packs on home life, social life, factory life—which included examples of industrial action led by women. They devised case studies of two men and two women with suitable questions for pupils' lines of enquiry. This material is now being published (**8**).

Infused courses

These are courses where the prime object of study may not be sexism, equal opportunities or the study of women but where these have been included as aspects of other topics. In this way, for instance, the topic of Law and Order might include work on women's as well as men's prisons; laws relating specifically to women; Acts of Parliament that effected changes in women's social or legal status, etc. A study of education in the nineteenth century might include a section on girls' and women's education, possibly tracing influences of this through to present-day attitudes to the education of women. This approach differs from the mere inclusion of content on women in that they are specifically studied, possibly making comparisons with the situation for men, or male viewpoints. If the emphasis is a positive one, such work can go some way towards compensating for a shortage of materials or course books which include women, at least until more are available (and the money to buy them with is, too). Some teachers draw on pupils' knowledge or ability to hypothesize and imagine situations and outcomes by setting creative assignments, such as writing imitation 'eye-witness accounts', 'letters home', 'newspaper reports' or stories and descriptions based upon actual events or topics studied. These exercises can be devised specifically to compensate for absences of women. They have the added advantage of requiring skills of empathy, comparison of several viewpoints, even developing critical skills used to detect bias.

Skills-based courses where teachers are particularly concerned to foster a wide range of skills in both sexes might need to include elements of compensatory education. Some schools have experimented with single-sex groups for encouraging specific skills, including mathematical and those related to personal and social development. One school gave favourabie accounts of single-sex assertiveness training, reporting that both boys and girls showed signs of increased confidence, cooperation within the peer group, and ease when discussing topics in small groups or full classes. Some pupils stated a preference for single-sex classes, other pupils enjoyed having just a few lessons this way.

Conclusion

The complex nature of this issue means that, ideally, it needs to be dealt with at many levels simultaneously. Although I have separated particular areas for discussion, each affects the others. For instance, the knowledge and experience available to staff and pupils in schools already developing policies on equal opportunities would provide a background to classroom discussion not available in schools with no such policy initiatives.

It is also an issue where it is important to retain openendedness and fluidity in order to attract thought and discussion at all levels. In this way, too, the varied experiences of pupils and teachers can add to the concepts as well as gain from them. It is an example of an issue where tentative, exploratory and critical discussion or writing is most evidently suitable because there are no 'experts'. Teaching methods and pupil responses need to be appropriate to these requirements.

5

Teaching Third World issues

Robert Stradling

Not-so-close encounters of the Third Kind
A survey of sixth-formers' comprehension of political concepts which was
conducted in 1973 revealed that only 13 per cent understood what was
usually meant by the term 'the Third World': the most common miscon-
ception was that it referred to 'the world to come'. For others it meant 'the
world after death'; 'the ideal social system—a form of Utopia'; 'war—the
end'; 'the belief of the Hindus in reincarnation'; and 'Nirvana' (1).

A study of adult attitudes towards overseas development and aid,
conducted five years later, revealed similar widespread ignorance. As
many people thought the term 'Third World' had something to do with
'Unidentified Flying Objects' and 'space travel' as thought it had to do
with 'world poverty' (2). However, it is also clear from this particular
study that ignorance is no bar to strong opinions and prejudices. The
survey tapped widespread latent and blatant xenophobia, stereotyping
and racism and a cluster of attitudes which the author of the report
characterized as national introversion—a total preoccupation with
Britain's domestic problems and an unwillingness or inability to relate
these problems to the global situation.

It is precisely this combination of strongly held opinions with a lack of
knowledge which is at the root of many of the difficulties confronting the
teacher dealing with Third World issues in the classroom. The intention
in this chapter therefore is to focus on some practical ways of coping with
this and a number of other related teaching problems, particularly in the
curriculum for 14–16-year-olds.

Third World issues in the curriculum

Increasingly teachers in secondary schools, and in a small but growing
number of primary and middle schools, are introducing topics in international relations, development, North–South, rich and poor countries,
and Third World issues in general into their curricula. Some schools now
offer courses in 'world studies' or 'development education' and indeed
some of the Examining Boards now offer syllabuses in development
studies for Ordinary and Advanced level. Some CSE Boards have also
sanctioned Mode 3 syllabuses with a similar emphasis. More typically,

however, Third World issues are likely to appear in geography, social studies and humanities.

These developments have received little official support. Admittedly in 1977 Shirley Williams, then Secretary of State for Education, stated in a Green Paper that 'We also live in a complex, interdependent world, and many of our problems in Britain require international solutions. The curriculum should therefore reflect our need to know about and understand other countries' (**3**). At the same time the Ministry for Overseas Development set up the Advisory Council of Development Education and a Development Education Fund to finance projects aimed at educating public opinion. But essentially the impetus for curriculum development in this field has come from teachers themselves, from privately funded projects such as the World Studies Project and from voluntary agencies such as Oxfam, the Centre for World Development Education, and Christian Aid. Indeed, some 38 voluntary agencies between them now produce or distribute about 1000 different educational packs, booklets, fact sheets and simulations specifically concerned with development and the Third World.

With so much material being produced by a wide variety of agencies and so many schools developing their own individual curriculum initiatives it is difficult to generalize. Nonetheless, a colleague, Eva Bennett, and I have tried to examine a range of materials and current practice in schools, and some trends are discernible:

1 Underlying most of the teaching material and much classroom teaching is a liberal humanist tradition. The emphasis is on international understanding and tolerance, mutual interests and cooperation. The value-position is perhaps epitomized by the widespread use of phrases such as 'global village', 'one world', and 'spaceship earth'.

2 There is a strong tendency for syllabuses and materials to focus on former colonies. Lessons on Africa and the Indian sub-continent predominate. As yet, not many teachers or voluntary agencies (CAFOD is one of the rare exceptions here) look at Latin America, China or South-East Asia.

3 There still tends to be a Eurocentric bias. At one time many geography and history textbooks were notorious for their Eurocentricity. The indigenous populations of Third World countries were presented as inadequate, unable to cope, the source of their own problems. Today the Eurocentric biases tend to be more subtle. In some cases the bias is revealed in the assumption that the most desirable and the most appropriate path for development is the Western one. In other instances the bias is apparent in the tendency to assume that all Third World countries are nation states in the Western European sense. Often children assume that the people in a Third World country share a common language, culture, history and way of life, thus overlooking the fact that such states are often merely the arbitrary creation of former colonial powers. Third World perspectives on global issues seldom get a hearing in either our own mass media or the available teaching materials. The emphasis on mutual interests and the 'global village' tends to avoid consideration of arguments from the South in favour of 'collective self-reliance' and independence from the constraints of Northern markets and Northern-based multi-national corporations.

4   Linked to the previous point is the equally widespread tendency to treat Third World issues in a rather ahistorical way. Although some syllabuses now include colonialism and imperialism as topics these are aspects of the past which tend to be overlooked in the materials and the teaching for younger age groups. And yet, without some historical background it is difficult to see how pupils can fully appreciate or explain the current political and economic relations between North and South or First and Third Worlds. Without some kind of historical context it is not surprising that one hears views from pupils such as, 'What's it got to do with us?'; 'Why should we have to help them?'; 'Charity begins at home!'.

5   The other trend which can be discerned in much of the material available and consequently in much classroom teaching is the tendency to examine relations between First World and Third World countries (aid, trade and cultural links) in a relatively apolitical way. The political aspirations of emerging nations, the close links between political and economic development, the global policies of the 'super powers', and the political influence of some multi-national corporations all need to be taken into account when considering North–South relations. Dudley Seers, in his review of Alan Hart's television film, *Five Minutes to Midnight*, high-lights the weaknesses of the apolitical approach to world development:

> One of the film's merits is that it may stimulate people to ask themselves whether the relief of world poverty is compatible with the maintenance of current life-styles . . . in countries already rich . . . (But) since there is no basic explanation of the state of the world, no overall strategy is implied for dealing with it. The message to the rich countries is that their citizens are in some way guilty. That they are guilty as individuals—and to purge that guilt they should indivi-dually consume less, support aid programmes, and give to charities. Such partial solutions could well be counter-productive, even if they were in fact widely adopted. A reduction in our consumption of food and beverages would make the poverty of many peasants still worse; aid is sometimes used to strengthen governments which are the chief obstacle to social development; charity can be a substitute) for real change . . . If one is serious about these matters, the question is one of politics, not individual action (**4**).

One can only speculate about the reasons for treating Third World issues in an apolitical way. In part I suspect it reflects the liberal humanist tradition but certainly another factor which should not be overlooked is the fact that schools rely heavily on voluntary agencies for teaching materials on the Third World. Most of these agencies are registered charities and one of the requirements of registration is that charities will not engage directly in political activity. Oxfam, for example, has been threatened with the loss of charitable status because its publications were thought to be becoming rather too political.

What is controversial about Third World issues?

It is symptomatic of some of the trends described above that it is even necessary to consider a question such as this. By comparison, issues such as Northern Ireland or nuclear disarmament seem more self-evidently controversial. To be fair, however, it is also the case that public opinion in Britain is neither greatly interested in Third World issues nor is it particularly divided regarding the causes or solutions of issues such as world poverty. Nevertheless, in global terms Third World issues are highly controversial and students should be encouraged to realize that their own assumptions are by no means self-evident.

To focus on development is to explore competing views of the good life. Mary Worrall, for example, defines development education in terms of 'educating children for change in a desirable direction', and this of course raises the whole question of what is and is not 'desirable'. The notion of 'education for change' is also potentially controversial whether one is talking about individual change—of attitudes, behaviour, and life-styles (or all three)—or social or political change. Furthermore, to focus on the historical and political contexts of North–South relations is to introduce potentially contentious issues relating to race, creed, colour, colonialism, neo-colonialism and exploitation, and these can be potentially divisive within the classroom, particularly in schools in multi-ethnic catchment areas. Whether this potential divisiveness is realized will depend to a large extent on the *way* in which teachers approach such issues, but it is difficult to see how justice can be done to the complexity and diversity of Third World relations with the developed North unless teachers address themselves to some of the following controversial issues.

Interdependence or dependence?
In recent years in the literature on development, particularly in the materials for schools, the concept of interdependence has loomed large. It is presented virtually as a moral imperative with the obvious implication that 'no man is an island'. In a general sense, the concept of global interdependence clearly characterizes the political and economic relationships between nations and between groups of nations. It implies that if

a change occurs in one part of the global system this will have implications throughout the entire system. Undoubtedly we have seen ample evidence of these inter-connections in the last two decades. One observer has described the relationship between the countries of the North during that period as, 'When Wall Street sneezes the European stock exchanges catch a cold'. Similarly, OPEC's decision to raise oil prices in the mid-'70s 'fuelled' inflation in the West, produced large increases in production costs, generated higher unemployment, produced a rapid fall in the demand for motor cars, and so forth. Western industrial economies suffered a downturn in the trade cycle. This in turn affected trade with the Third World, and if the London Stock Exchange was suffering from a cold then some Third World economies had caught the economic equivalent of double pneumonia.

Undoubtedly, then, Third World countries depend on developed economies to supply them with machinery, technical expertise, financial credits and access to markets for their raw materials and semi-processed products. Likewise Western countries could be said to be dependent on Third World countries to supply them with raw materials, foodstuffs, oil and other scarce resources and to provide them with markets for their own manufactured goods.

However, critics of the concept of interdependence, particularly critics from the Third World, claim that there is an important qualitative difference between their dependence on the North and the North's dependence on the South. It is the Northern countries, they argue, which have the power to make the rules governing the global economy, and have the power to take initiatives rather than merely react to changing political and economic circumstances. The role of the International Monetary Fund is an interesting case in point. To counter Southern criticisms one could point to the Labour Government's experience in Britain in the 1970s when in return for financial assistance the IMF insisted on important changes in the Government's economic and fiscal policies. On the other hand, critics from the South could respond to this that at least the British Government helps to shape the rules of the IMF. Britain along with the USA, West Germany, France and Japan virtually determine IMF policy between them since the voting system is deliberately weighted in their favour (**5**).

How did global inequality come about? Who is responsible?
It is often argued that we should not dwell on the past when teaching about the Third World. This only creates negative feelings and a sense of guilt and may be counter-productive. So, instead, teachers are recommended to stress the gains which *we* in the North can make if there is a concerted effort to reduce inequalities in the world. But it could be argued that the absence of any attempt to examine critically the implications of

colonialism will encourage a perspective in which the state of Third World countries is seen as 'natural'—akin to our level of development one hundred years ago.

The alternative is to focus on how the present pattern of poorer Third World countries mainly supplying raw materials and semi-processed products to the North is left over from colonial days. That is to say, the development of transport systems reflected the colonial powers' concern with military security and the problems of exporting raw materials rather than a concern with linking the various regions of a country. Agriculture was developed to facilitate production for export. Local financing and investment in new enterprises were often actively discouraged. In such circumstances it is perhaps not surprising that the South's share of manufactured exports is still very small (10%), nor perhaps is it surprising that the countries of the South are calling for a New International Economic Order.

How can global inequalities best be eradicated?
It is clear that there is a considerable controversy here. Governments of Northern countries are divided on this as are significant pressure groups such as multi-national corporations and trade unions. Southern countries are also divided on this issue. Essentially there are three competing positions:

   i)   Reagan/Thatcher conservatism argues that the North must first 'put its own house in order' by reducing public expenditure (including aid), getting a grip on inflation, high interest rates and falling productivity. This will restore stability and economic growth in the global economy and this in turn will help the economies of the Third World;

   ii)   the Neo-Keynesian approach of the Brandt Commission is to prime the pump in Southern economies through a transfer of resources from the rich countries of the First and Second Worlds. This will be mutually beneficial since it will increase the supply of raw materials needed in the North and stimulate demand in the South for Northern manufactured products;

   iii)   collective self-reliance or South–South cooperation in which the countries of the South extricate themselves from their current trading relations with the North or protect themselves from Northern exploitation. Strategy here includes the setting up of equivalents to the Common Market (e.g. the Latin American Integration Association); regional trade agreements; the development of regional producer cartels (e.g. for sugar, textiles, natural fibres, etc.); a Southern-based financial system such as a Third-World Bank; and so forth.

Why is the proportion of absolute poor in the Third World increasing in spite of governments, international agencies and development experts spending the last two development decades on attempting to eradicate this?

Conventional wisdom attributes this trend to three factors: i) A high rate of population growth in the Third World; ii) the large increase in oil prices in the mid-'70s; iii) world recession. But many Southern governments and the political Left in the North counter this by asking why population growth should be a major problem when statistics show that there is ample food to go round and the problem is distribution, not production. These critics also point to the fact that many developing countries have experienced comparatively high rates of economic growth but are starting from essentially a very low base. It has been calculated, for example, that although Brazil has enjoyed a high growth rate of 9 per cent throughout the 1970s, it would take 362 years at that rate to close the per capita income gap with the rich countries of the world even assuming that the economic situation in the latter remains static during that time. Shridath Ramphal, Secretary-General of the Commonwealth Secretariat, has stated this position as follows:

> At the end of three decades of international action devoted to development the result by 1985 is likely to be an increase of 50 dollars per capita in the annual incomes of the poorest group (of countries), compared with an increase of 3900 for those of the richest who were already, in 1965, 3000 per cent better off (**6**).

It has also been pointed out that the gap between rich and poor within most Third World countries has also been widening during the last two decades since the benefits obtained from development have not 'trickled down' to the poor.

Appropriate strategies for development

The early development programmes were aimed at transforming 'backward' economies by wholesale importation of machinery, technical expertise and capital to bring about modernization. The emphasis also was, and still is, on export-led growth. Whether or not the benefits of such a strategy outweigh the costs is a contentious issue. Supporters of the strategy point to the success stories like Hong Kong, Singapore and Taiwan. Critics point to the failures and emphasize in particular the fact that absolute poverty is increasing even in developing countries with a high economic growth rate. They advocate the need for a different strategy, one which would produce more jobs, operate more at the rural level in order to stem the tide of migration to the cities and shanty towns, and will be geared to self-help and the development of new, purpose-designed technologies.

Why should Britain open its markets to cheap imports and thereby increase unemployment in our own industries?
The Brandt Commission called for the removal of protectionist barriers in the North. Conservative monetarists in the West share that belief in the market and free trade but are not averse to the imposition of tariffs on the import of manufactured goods and processed products from the Third World. Trade unions in the Northern countries call for import controls to protect jobs and stave off a balance-of-payments crisis. In some cases they support a straight import-control policy, in other cases unionists and the political Left argue for some industrial re-adjustment to changing economic conditions and selective import controls which would ensure preferential access to our markets for the least developed countries. The argument here usually is that it is countries like Japan and the newly industrialized countries (e.g. Hong Kong, Taiwan, South Korea, etc.) which pose the greatest threat to jobs in Britain.

Should aid to Third World countries be tied to the purchase of our goods and services?
Conservative administrations in Europe and the United States have no doubts about this. At present two-thirds of British aid is 'tied' in this way. This position has been affirmed by the British government: 'We believe it is right at the present time to give greater weight in the allocation of our aid to political, industrial and commercial considerations alongside our basic developmental objectives' (speech by the Minister for Overseas Development, 1980). Critics from the South tend to argue that 'tied' aid forces the receiver to mortgage its future and become economically and politically dependent on the donor, and often forces the recipient to buy over-priced goods and unsuitable technology rather than develop its own domestic industry and skills. Critics in the North have raised doubts about all forms of tied aid and bilateral aid (i.e. between donor country and a specific recipient). On the far Right critics argue that aid removes the obligation on investors and governments in Third World countries to generate resources locally and devise their own policies for development. On the Left, critics reiterate Southern fears about aid reinforcing dependence and argue that it tends to enrich a small proportion of the population but does little to relieve poverty and often delays necessary economic and political changes in Third World countries.

Political interference by the superpowers
An increasingly contentious issue in the South arises out of the growing tendency of the superpowers to interfere in the political affairs of Third World countries. This interference may be to uphold a friendly regime, e.g. El Salvador or Afghanistan, or it may be to overthrow an unfriendly regime (e.g. Chile, Nicaragua, Ethiopia or South Yemen). This may be done by direct military intervention, or by economic sanctions or by the

use of third parties (large multi-national corporations in the case of the United States, Cuba in the case of the USSR). Regardless of method, this whole issue raises serious questions about sovereignty, independence, and the right to self-determination—fine phrases which the superpowers are very fond of using.

'Westernization'

Public opinion in the North often takes it for granted that Third World countries wish to follow our direction and develop along similar lines. Contentious issues underlying this whole notion of Westernization include:

> *'Coca-colonization'*   The process of using high-powered advertising in Third World countries to boost demand for such essential manu-factured products of western civilization as Coca-Cola, jeans, sun-glasses, 50 cc motor bikes, etc.;

> *Medicine*   Attempts to export prevailing Western patterns of medicine and health care (e.g. bottle- rather than breast-feeding of babies), combined with the use of Third World countries as testing grounds for drugs which are banned in the North;

> *Technology*   The export of technology which may not be appropriate for the recipient country's level of development. A current issue here is whether the micro-technology industries in the North will seek to export Northern consumption patterns (e.g. demand for video games), or seek to meet the actual requirements of Third World conditions.

> *Erosion of cultural values*   A growing complaint in the South about the effects of Westernization. This, for example, has clearly fuelled the rise of Islamic fundamentalism.

Human rights

In terms of North–South relations this is a threefold issue. The first question is, do the economic policies of the developed countries infringe the rights of the citizens of Third World countries? In liberal democracies we tend to associate 'human rights' with civil and political rights (the right to vote, a free press, freedom of speech and association). Less concern is expressed about what the United Nations refers to as economic and social rights (freedom from hunger, poverty and disease, the right to fair employment, etc.). According to critics of Western policy these rights imply a fairer share of the world's resources *between* North and South and *within* Third World countries, and on both counts the policies of Western governments and multi-national corporations tend to maintain rather than eradicate such inequalities.

Second, do the political policies of developed countries infringe on the civil and political rights of the citizens of Third World countries? A reference here to the tendency of Western governments and multi-national corporations to prefer political stability in the Third World even if the price for that stability is dictatorship, torture and arbitrary imprisonment, and widespread infringement of rights.

Finally, should a Western donor country cut off aid to a developing country which is clearly denying the civil and political rights of its citizens? Here we have the other side of the coin to the previous point. Some Western countries such as Sweden do pursue this sort of policy although it is perhaps significant that they tend not to be former colonial powers. Britain has only tended to adopt this sort of policy in extreme circumstances; for example, aid was cut off to Amin's Uganda.

The role and power of multi-national corporations in the Third World
No doubt some readers will have had the experience of obtaining information from multi-national corporations about their activities in Third World countries and will have received glossy brochures about the benefits accruing to the host country, for example, the injection of much-needed capital, technological know-how, management skills, employment, and so on. Indeed you will have to search hard to find any reference to profit. Increasingly, Third World countries are talking about the need for effective regulation of multi-national corporations' activities partly because they often exercise monopolistic power over prices and profits, avoid taxation, and make economic decisions on a global rather than a national basis; but also this is partly because some multi-national corporations have been known to interfere in the politics of Third World states. There are a number of well-documented cases of multi-national corporations doing precisely this, for example, the payment of bribes to senior officials by the Lockheed Corporation; the involvement of ITT in the overthrow of the Allende regime in Chile; the illegal supply of oil to Rhodesia by the large oil companies. Information about such activities is not easy to get hold of but is essential if teaching about multi-national corporations is going to be balanced and is going to explain why their role in the world is not always seen as wholly beneficent by the populations of Third World countries.

If there are sufficient foodstuffs to feed adequately every person on earth (World Bank Report 1980), then why are people starving?
The problem would appear to be one of distribution rather than production, as pointed out earlier. Any consideration of this issue inevitably raises additional questions.

  –food consumption patterns in the North; i.e. basic human foods in the Third World (e.g. cereals) are used in large amounts in the

North as animal food in order to maintain a high rate of meat
consumption;

—even if there are adequate supplies of foodstuffs this does not mean
that everyone can afford them;

—the policies of governments in the North often artificially push up
the prices of food. From time to time United States governments
have paid American farmers not to grow produce; the EEC's
Common Agricultural Policy can lead to surpluses in some products
(e.g. butter mountains, milk lakes) and shortages in others;

—food stocks, like other commodities, are the subject of speculation on
the exchanges of Western economies leading to wide fluctuations of
prices;

—Third World countries which used to be self-sufficient in food now
have to import it because their agricultural production has shifted
to cash crops for sale to the North in exchange for foreign currency;

—the Green Revolution has led to spectacular improvements in yields
in some parts of the world (e.g. India), but has had less impact in
others (including Africa), partly because technical improvement
has only affected the large farmers and the lack of political will to
initiate land reform has led to the persistence of conditions which
are not conducive to much-needed changes in agriculture.

Clearly no list of controversial issues relating to the Third World can be
comprehensive. However, the issues referred to earlier should demonstrate why teaching about the Third World can be contentious on a global
scale (between First and Third Worlds, North and South, developed and
developing countries). Within Britain these issues can also be controversial, dividing Conservatives, Liberals, Socialists and Marxists; and,
since we are inevitably dealing in the classroom with alternative sets of
values about who is responsible for the current situation, who is most
adversely affected, what should be done about it, and so on, this is also an
issue which can upset parents, local politicians and school governors. It is
not that long ago that Basil Davidson's school textbook *Africa*, published
by Longman, was debated in the House of Lords because of its radical
content. Whilst the controversial nature of these issues may create
problems for individual teachers it should be stressed that to teach about
the Third World as if there were no controversies at all would be either to
perpetuate a particular ideological view of the world or to distort the
content of lessons.

Potential teaching problems

In this section of the chapter I shall be considering some of the main
pedagogic problems which can confront the teacher when introducing
Third World issues into social studies or humanities courses for the 14–16

year age range. Then in the following section, I shall go on to discuss the potential and relative advantages and disadvantages of some of the approaches and methods teachers now use, or those which have been advocated by curriculum developers.

The emphasis here is very much on *potential* problems. I am not asserting that such problems are inevitable in every classroom. By no means every teacher is going to be faced by a consensus of ethnocentric and xenophobic reactions to the cultures and experiences of people who happen to live to the south of Land's End—but many will. Nor do all of these potential teaching problems arise directly out of the controversial nature of Third World issues. An inability to handle abstract concepts, for example, is a problem likely to arise in most subject areas of the curriculum. However, unless an adequate means is found of coping with a problem like this it is highly unlikely that pupils will be able to grasp why Third World issues are highly controversial and why people cannot agree about the kinds of questions raised in the previous section.

For the sake of convenience the potential problems have been grouped into five broad categories:

1 *Capturing the interest of 14–16-year-olds* on issues which they may not perceive as having any relevance to their own lives, and on topics such as 'The Third World' or 'North–South' which are both conceptually and geographically remote.

2 *Encouraging young people to question their taken-for-granted attitudes, prejudices, preconceptions and assumptions* regarding Third World countries and their relations with Britain and the other developed countries of the North. There are at least four categories of attitude or assumption which present problems when teaching Third World issues:

    i)   A battery of attitudes including stereotyping ('lazy peasants in Latin America', 'primitive natives brandishing spears in Africa'), ethnocentrism, a tendency to be patronizing and paternalistic, and even outbursts of xenophobia. As Mary Worrall says, 'Tarzan has a lot to answer for!' (**7**). Clearly such attitudes can be a major constraint on learning.

    ii)   A tendency to use British culture and social, political and economic practices and institutions as a yardstick for measuring not only the development but also the level of civilization in other countries.

    iii)   Preconceptions that pupils have about other countries based on their knowledge of their own country, for example, that the indigenous population all speak the same language, that the nuclear family is typical, that the state has a health service, that old people get pensions, etc.

    iv)   The application of certain traditional modes and habits of

Western thinking to the study of the Third World which can have unfortunate implications and consequences. For example, one component of the Western tradition is the tendency to impose a rank order on diversity. Nature, for example, is viewed as a series of hierarchies and biology textbooks emphasize the higher and lower orders of species. Human beings are often assumed to be the managers or 'stewards' of the planet rather than just one more species as totally dependent on the cycles of the biosphere for our existence as all the other species. One experienced geographer observed to me that many of his pupils seemed to see the peoples of Third World countries as being 'lower down the evolutionary ladder than themselves'. Another related component is the tendency to reduce diversity into dichotomies: good/bad, for/against, either/or, them/us (**8**).

3   *Conveying the political and economic complexities of Third World issues.* Most of the controversial issues outlined in the previous section of this chapter are highly complex. With mixed-ability groupings in particular, it is difficult to get pupils to see how a Third World government's freedom of decision and action can be curtailed by a wide variety of factors, e.g. its dependency on outside agencies and countries for aid, markets, imports, financial assistance and technical expertise; the expectations of its own peoples; the degree of cultural diversity or homogeneity; the size of the population; the power of multi-national corporations operating inside the country; relations with neighbouring countries; whether or not it is within the sphere of influence of one of the superpowers; and so forth. The problem, then, is how to do justice to the complexity of the issues without confusing pupils to the point where they 'switch off', or opt for simplistic explanations and solutions.

4   *Helping pupils to grasp the abstractions and concepts which are central to an understanding of Third World issues.* The Third World itself is a concept, or rather a series of interrelated concepts. Thus, while over 90 countries are commonly referred to as Third World nations, the basic differences between them are often greater than the similarities. Some are democracies, some are military dictatorships, yet others are still feudal. Geographically most are located in the South but not all states in the Southern hemisphere could be regarded as Third World countries. Some have been politically independent for less than 30 years, others, particularly in Latin America, have been independent for over 150 years. So in many respects the Third World is a rather intangible concept and yet it has considerable descriptive and analytical power. Other concepts such as development, dependency, and interdependence are also highly abstract yet equally useful in trying to understand Third World issues. The problem, therefore, is how best to make them concrete without losing their essential value as a means of generalizing about the world.

5 *Handling controversial subject matter.* It was earlier noted that there is a kind of liberal humanist consensus underpinning much of the teaching material and classroom practice on Third World issues. But liberal humanist solutions and explanations of events and issues are rejected by other political groups in the North and by some Third World countries and groups. In the light of the previous problem, then, the problem here is threefold:

–Is a committed line on Third World issues legitimate or justifiable?
–Could a committed line be counter-productive?
–How can pupils be encouraged to think for themselves?

Teaching approaches and methods

The concern here is with strategies which teachers can adopt in order to circumvent or at least minimize the problems outlined in the previous section. In discussing the efficacy of some of these approaches I shall draw on the observations and experience of Ian Pearce, a geographer and Head of Social Studies at Tamworth Manor High School, Merton. Ian teaches Third World issues to pupils in the 13–16 age range at this school and has done so in the past at schools in other parts of London including Tottenham and Southall. He has had experience of teaching classes made up almost entirely of children from ethnic minorities, classes in which all the various communities have been equally represented, and classes which are predominantly Anglo-Saxon.

Entry points

Many teachers find it useful to start off a unit of lessons on the Third World with some method of finding out what pupils already know and think about the key issues. This could be a knowledge test to find out if they can name some leaders of Third World countries, or name some of Britain's former colonies in Africa or Asia, etc. Alternatively, the questionnaire could focus on pupils' views regarding 'What are the major problems facing the world today?' or tap their attitudes, e.g. 'What things do you tend to think of when the word Africa (Asia, Latin America, Middle East, etc.) is mentioned?' A questionnaire like this could also be used to get pupils to rank order a set of statements about why countries are poor (e.g. bad government, difficult climate, exploitation by rich countries, overpopulation, etc.).

Another way of tapping pupils' attitudes and impressions is to offer them a blank map of the world and ask them to describe what they associate with the different regimes of the world or even a specific country.

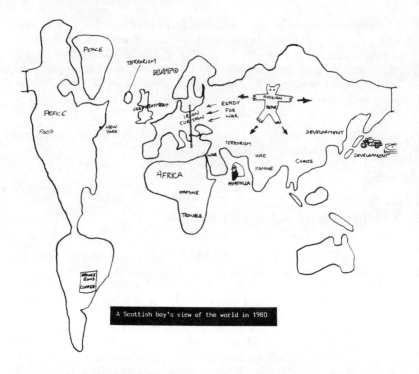

A Scottish boy's view of the world in 1980

The illustration above is taken from a booklet called *Interdependence* produced by the Jordanhill Project in International Understanding. It illustrates one Scottish pupil's mental images of different countries.

Fairly early on in the unit of lessons some decision has to be taken about how to deal with the problem of teaching about countries and problems which may be conceptually and geographically remote from the everyday experiences of children in a typical British classroom. This is a problem which has long exercised the ingenuity of geographers. This contrasts with the trend in recent years in much social studies and humanities teaching—and the trend is even more pronounced in newer subject areas such as social and political education—to focus, at least initially, on the pupil's immediate environment and direct experiences. 'Relevance' has been the keyword.

One approach which is employed increasingly in development education is to start with a case study of the pupils' locality. As the Birmingham Development Education Centre puts it:

> Birmingham is also 'developing'. Decisions are being made at many
> levels based not only on local interests, but also on 'outside

influences' such as world markets, aid to Birmingham and investment, all of which determine the priorities for Birmingham's
development. Reflection on this led to the idea that a study of these
priorities, the complexity of the numerous factors influencing
decisions, the predominant interests reflected in policy and where
decisions are made, could be a useful introduction to a study of
development dilemmas in other places (**10**).

A group of pupils looking at their locality in this way could examine any
or all of the following questions:

—What forms of 'aid' does our town, locality or region receive? (e.g.
  EEC regional grants and loans, urban renewal grants, Government
  Development grants, etc.)
—Is the town or region designated as a development area?
—What local evidence do we have of the need for development? (e.g.
  high unemployment, dilapidated schools, lack of recreation
  facilities, slums, traffic bottlenecks, overcrowded housing, etc.)
—What local signs are there of development? (slum clearance, new
  buildings, new housing estates, improved services, provision for
  population overspill, new factories, etc.)
—What is the role of non-governmental agencies in local development?
—What are the policies and priorities of the decision makers? (e.g.
  structure plans, development proposals, etc.)
—How do the local inhabitants respond to these plans and proposals
  for development?
—Who are the major private investors in the locality?
—Are any local firms subsidiaries of major multi-national
  corporations?
—Are production and planning decisions taken locally or are they
  taken in London, New York, Tokyo or Hamburg?

The idea that we are all involved in development processes and that our
influence and freedom of choice may be limited by 'outside factors' is
central to this approach. Equally important is the notion that students
should be presented with situations and experiences which parallel the
situations and experiences of people in Third World countries. This is not
the same thing as presenting them with *identical* experiences. The
contrasts will be as significant as the similarities. Ian Pearce points this
out when describing one of the first lessons in his unit on the Third
World:

We use films, we've used speakers. This year I brought in a guy who
had taught in Tanzania for a year. He described a day in a Tanzanian
school. That's concrete and it's parallel. The fact that school begins

at 6.00 a.m., they often have to get their own breakfast, and they spend time making clothes which are then shared out. And then there's a whole load of functional things; the school has its own farm and the kids spend three hours of the day on the farm to provide food for school dinners. That really hits our kids. They know about school dinners. There's a parallel experience. That was very important for us. The visitor had photographs of the Tanzanian children at school, and information about the curriculum. Practical lessons on types of soil, fertilizer, and so on. There isn't much time in the curriculum for formal academic study—art and poetry, for example—because they've only got a few years to work with. All that had a clear impact on our children and was very useful.

The case for sticking with pupils' own experience of development and with parallels and contrasts is a strong one, particularly if children's knowledge of the Third World and interest in Third World issues is very low. But Michael Storm's counter-argument is worth bearing in mind and may match some readers' own experiences:

> If we really believe in starting from the child's own interests, we often find that he(sic) is, awkwardly enough, much more interested in volcanoes, Australian aboriginals, coral islands, than in plotting the distribution of lamp posts or making a map of the cycle sheds (11).

Perhaps the best way to link the two alternative standpoints here is initially to focus on controversial issues which have been thrown up by a questionnaire or some similar activity. If strong feelings are expressed about Britain's contribution to aid programmes, for example, then this might be the ideal starting-point, particularly if one demonstrates the forms of aid which Britain (or even the locality) receives.

Pupils' attitudes

There are attitudes based on ignorance and lack of contact, and there are attitudes and assumptions which are essentially cultural. Generally speaking, it is possible to present pupils with facts and alternative perspectives which might at least encourage them to question both types of attitude even if this does not lead to changes in perspective. The third kind of attitude is more firmly fixed and also more intensely held. Such attitudes perform some kind of psychological function for those who hold them. Xenophobia is a case in point. It is commonly defined as a morbid fear and distrust of foreigners and does not necessarily diminish through personal contact. Similarly, racist attitudes may serve as a kind of ego defence mechanism for some young people and consequently lessen their own sense of inferiority. Such attitudes are unlikely to be changed or even brought into question by two periods per week of Third World studies in the fourth year.

Taking these potential limitations into account, it is still possible to adopt a number of strategies and methods which can encourage pupils to examine critically their own and other people's attitudes. Some of the approaches already discussed under *Entry points* are useful here, including mental maps, questionnaires—students designing their own questionnaires can be a useful way of examining the nature of prejudice—and exploring stereotypes through looking at photographs (e.g. which photograph best illustrates your idea of Africa, and why?).

Another approach used to good effect by some teachers is to encourage pupils to see themselves as others see them. Ann Hurman's school textbook *As others see us* gets pupils to examine critically their own values and attitudes through looking at other countries' stereotypical images of the British (**12**). Roger Shipton-Smith has suggested that teachers can counter the 'funny peculiar' reactions of many pupils to the habits and behaviours of people from other countries by adopting a kind of anthropological way of looking at their own society. Looking, for example, at patterns of behaviour, values and habits which might be thought peculiar by other people (**13**).

An interesting variation on this approach is to collect quotes which offer a Third World perspective. Ideally the quotations should be selected for their provocativeness and pupils can be asked to discuss their reactions to such observations. Examples of this type of quote are provided below.

> We have held, and we still hold, that Africa's gift to world culture must be in the field of Human Relations. . . . The experts have all kinds of standards by which they judge the degree of civilization of a people. In the African traditional Society the test is this. How does that Society treat its old people and, indeed, all its members who are not useful and productive in the narrowest sense? Judged by this standard, the so-called advanced societies have a lot to learn which the so-called backward societies could teach them.
> *Dr. Kenneth Kaunda*

> Nowhere would we find better instances of keeping land scrupulously clear from weeds, of ingenuity in device of water-raising appliances, of knowledge of soils and their capabilities, as well as of the exact time to sow and reap, as one would find in Indian agriculture. It is wonderful too, how much is known of rotation, the system of 'mixed crops' and of fallowing. . . . I, at least, have never seen a more perfect picture of cultivation.
> *A. J. Voelker*, a Dutch agricultural scientist in India in the 1890s.

> *Reporter:*   Mr Gandhi, what do you think of Western civilization?
> *Gandhi:*   I think it would be a good idea.

There is also a tendency for pupils to exhibit more prejudice towards countries which have ex-colonial associations. When prejudices are strong and widespread in the class it might be better to focus on regions of the Third World about which they have fewer preconceptions, such as Latin America and South East Asia.

However, perhaps a cautionary note is in order here. Encouraging students to appreciate that people in Third World countries are not stupid, or unable to cope, and that they may have developed their own solutions to problems which are more effective than ours, and may be constrained from being more effective because of decisions taken in First World countries, may counter some of the ignorance which is rife. It need not necessarily erode their prejudices. An Australian teacher has vividly portrayed the problem:

> The views of one pupil were expressed as 'Forinners is stoopid Bastuds', which aptly summed up the general attitude of the class. Over the next few weeks, the class was exposed to books and films which emphasized some of the achievements and abilities of various foreigners. At the end of the period the same student's attitude had changed to 'Forinners is cunnin Bastuds' (**14**).

Comparing political and economic complexities

QUESTIONS FOR PUPILS	BRITAIN	TANZANIA
For each country: 1 Does it have its own supplies of oil and coal? 2 Does it need to import food? 3 What goods and raw materials does it spend most money on importing? (List no more than five.) 4 Which countries are the main suppliers of these imports? 5 What are its main exports? (List no more than five.) 6 Which countries are the leading customers for these exports? 7 Does it trade with both superpowers? 8 Is its government committed to the international policies of *one* of the superpowers? Which one? 9 Does a superpower have military, naval or air bases in either country? 10 How much foreign aid does it receive? (Give the total amount of aid per year, and the average amount of aid per person per year.) 11 Who are the main givers of this aid? 12 What is the country's relationship with the aid givers? (e.g. an ex-colony, member of a trade group, ally, etc.)		

Political and economic complexities

Clearly, what one can achieve here depends on the time at one's disposal, the age of the pupils, and their cognitive ability. I have assumed throughout this chapter that most teachers will be thinking in terms of a unit or module of lessons on the Third World—at best a term, more likely half a term.

In such circumstances there is a strong case for focusing on certain basic ideas. The notion of choice, in particular, ought to be explored since it is at the heart of most Third World issues. On the one hand there is the problem of choosing priorities for development. For example, which is preferable: a fast rate of economic growth or a fairer distribution of wealth, benefits and other resources? Should they use foreign aid on prestigious projects which will raise the country's standing in the world and might attract further foreign investment or use it to alleviate poverty? What should have priority: rapid industrialization or an extension of civil rights and political development? Should the property, equipment, land rights and other assets owned by foreign companies be expropriated by the new state or should more foreign corporations be encouraged to invest in the country?

Determining priorities is one important component of choice here. But pupils also need to understand the other side of the coin. That is, to what extent the Third World government's 'freedom to choose' is curtailed. A government's 'room for manoeuvre' and relative independence or dependence will clearly have an important impact on its decisions and on its ability to implement its policies.

The key problem for the teacher is how to convey such ideas in a reasonably intelligible and simple (but not simplistic) way. A useful starting-point here can be to examine the relative dependency of two countries, one of which should be Britain and the other a Third World country on which there is ample and readily accessible information, e.g. Kenya, Tanzania, Brazil, Peru, Jamaica or India. Pupils, singly or in small groups, are then asked to find out information directly from reference sources or from a worksheet in order to complete a table similar to the one opposite. Pupils can be asked for single-word answers such as yes/no or the name of a key export or import, and simple statistics.

The purpose of the exercise is twofold:

a)   to demonstrate that Britain as well as the Third World country is dependent on other countries in a variety of ways;
b)   to indicate that Britain probably has more room for manoeuvre.

Case studies are another useful approach here. A number of books and packs listed in the bibliography provide useful case studies of difficult political and economic choices facing Third World countries (**15**). The problem of development can often be highlighted by looking at countries where the room to manoeuvre is severely curtailed by political and geographical factors, e.g. landlocked countries like Lesotho or Upper Volta, and countries where freedom of action and choice could be highly constrained but this does not appear to have adversely affected economic development (e.g. Hong Kong or South Korea). For example, a map showing the southern half of Africa vividly illustrates Lesotho's problems. Small and completely surrounded by South Africa, Lesotho is likely to find that its policy options are few and constrained by its neighbour. Being landlocked it is dependent on South Africa for access to ports and markets and for power supplies. It is clearly vulnerable to military invasion, trade boycotts and sanctions, trade penetration by South Africa, and the cutting of communications with the outside world. If sufficient background material can be collected it might be interesting to contrast Lesotho with another landlocked country to the north of South Africa—Zimbabwe—and explain the factors (geographical, political and economic) which make Zimbabwe less dependent than Lesotho on her southern neighbour.

Case studies of multi-national corporations could also be a useful way in to considering development issues. The Birmingham Development Education Centre, for example, suggests that pupils could take a locally based multi-national corporation and conduct a case study of its operations—in which countries it operates, the products it manufactures, its subsidiaries, whether MNC controls all aspects of the goods it manufactures (raw materials, processing, manufacturing, marketing) and so on (**10**). The information can be collected from company publicity, *Kompass*, and *Who owns Whom*. The latter two are likely to be in the reference section of the local library.

The case study using the enquiry-based approach is one strategy for exploring the political and economic implications of development choices. Another approach is to use one or more of the games and simulations now available. The Birmingham DEC's publication *Priorities for Development* (**10**) includes details of a game devised by post-graduate students from Birmingham University based on the experience of the BSA motorcycle company. As managing directors of the company, players have to cope with a whole range of factors and events which influence the company's future. These include:

> 'The US government decides to ban your bike because it causes pollution.'
> 'Dock strike prevents access to some of your parts.'
> 'Exports affected by strength of the £.'

Another simulation which offers a great deal of scope is reproduced in *Development Studies: A Handbook for Teachers* (**13**). This is a simulation of the Cabinet of a West African state meeting to discuss a proposal from a British firm to build a new factory in their country.

Although it may be time-consuming it is also possible to devise variations around this basic theme. The skeleton of one of these variations is described opposite.

SIERRA DE COBRE: A SIMULATION

Background: Sierra de Cobre is an imaginary country in South America. Two-thirds of the foreign currency it earns comes from the sale of copper. It also exports small amounts of other minerals including nickel and lead, and is a small exporter of coffee beans. The country has few energy resources of its own and depends on the import of oil from OPEC countries and natural gas from Venezuela. Although 30 per cent of the workforce are in agriculture they do not produce enough food to be self-sufficient. The country therefore imports cereals and wheat from the USA and Brazil. After a series of revolutions and counter-revolutions, and occasional periods of democratic stability, the country was ruled by a military dictatorship. However, two years ago a national election was held (the first for 25 years) in which the Popular United Front (a coalition of left-wing parties) defeated the right-wing party, the People's Democratic Party, by a small majority.

The problem: Because of the world recession the price for copper has fallen, the prices of key imports (food and oil) have risen. Inflation has increased and some of the mines have been temporarily closed by the owners, International Mining Incorporated, a US corporation. Unemployment is rising rapidly, US banks refuse to extend further credit to the Sierra de Cobre government. The Cabinet approaches the International Monetary Fund for a loan, and the IMF agrees but only if the government reduces its current expenditure on social and educational reforms, drops future plans for further public expenditure, and drops the idea of a guaranteed minimum wage for all workers.

The players:
   The Cabinet: The Popular United Front was elected to bring about a greater redistribution of wealth; large wage increases for mine workers and a minimum guaranteed wage for all; financial assistance to farmers; improvements in health and welfare provision for the old, the handicapped and the unemployed; and better education (40 per cent of the population are illiterate). To begin with, the government has financed some of these reforms through large loans from foreign (mainly US) banks which already had investments in Sierra de Cobre. The government intends nationalizing the foreign-owned copper mines to use the profits to pay higher wages and finance further social and economic reforms. The Cabinet is now meeting to make two decisions:
      1   Should the government reverse some of its reforms (particularly the increases in public expenditure and the decision to bring in a guaranteed minimum wage) in order to get financial assistance from the IMF?
      2   Should the government nationalize the foreign-owned copper mines?
International Mining Incorporated: The present owners of the copper mines in Sierra de Cobre. Anxious about the intention of the government to nationalize the mines, the IMI Board of Directors meets to decide what actions they can take to stop this happening.
National Mine Workers Union: Although the NMWU is now officially recognized by the government (it was banned under the military regime), the Executive of the Union is dissatisfied with the present situation in the country. Wages have not increased as much as expected, and they are worried about the levels of unemployment and inflation. The Executive is also concerned that if the Cabinet agrees to demands of the IMF then the mine workers will be as badly off as they were before the election. There are calls from rank-and-file members of the Union to join with other Trade Unions in a national strike. The Executive is meeting to decide what to do.
'The rebels': This is a group of right-wing army officers who disapproved of the decision to hold a general election and are now concerned about the growing political and economic crisis. The rebel officers, on manoeuvres in the remote

north of the country, have led a mutiny of the troops in the 1st and 5th brigades.
They are now considering their next action.

Notes
It is possible to introduce other groups into the simulation including the IMF, the
US Government, and the PDP Opposition, or the teacher can take on these roles
and make suggestions to and form coalitions with the various players. The
teacher as 'controller' can also introduce a series of 'wild cards' to present further
problems and crises: e.g.
   'News has just come through of fighting on the border with Chaco.'
   'The US Government threatens trade sanctions if Sierra de Cobre nationalizes
   the copper mines.'
   'Cuba offers the government military assistance to deal with the rebel elements
   in the army.'

Abstract concepts

Many concepts relating to the Third World and development issues are
simply unfamiliar to pupils rather than highly abstract and demanding.
For example, *neo-colonialism*, *diversification* and *gross national product* are
essentially useful labels which can be taught as one would teach other
unfamiliar labels in other subjects. But some concepts, clearly, are highly
abstract ideas and they will always be difficult to teach, especially to the
less able pupil. Concepts such as *interdependence*, *development* and *structural
violence*, for example, are difficult to grasp. To quote Ian Pearce again:

> To understand the complexity of the interdependence between the
> developed and developing worlds takes such a high cognitive level of
> understanding that it may be too demanding for some kids. You need
> to make the abstract concept concrete for them and that is difficult
> with a concept like global interdependence. You can illustrate
> village-to-village interdependence on a concrete scale but the global
> scale needs a high level of cognitive ability.

It is often argued that for students to understand a concept like 'global
interdependence' they have to consider such questions as:

Where do I fit in?
In what ways do I depend on others?
In what ways do others depend on me?

Both Birmingham DEC and the World Studies Project argue for this
approach (**16**). The former suggests, for example, starting with the various
trade and economic connections involved in obtaining sugar for a cup of
tea. They also favour the use of topic webs and networks so that pupils can
see all the connections and see complicated issues as a whole rather than
as unrelated fragments. This approach is shown opposite by an example
of one of these topic webs. One way of generating such webs might be
through brainstorming activities by small groups of pupils; another is to

get pupils to 'translate' a written description into a graphic representation. A third approach is for the teacher, using a blackboard or OHP,
gradually to build up a network or web by exploring the connections as
one goes (**17**).

The main problem with a web like the one illustrated is that it is static.
With a concept such as interdependence it is not really the connections
that are important, but the dynamic processes going on. What is needed
really is to introduce a change factor into a diagram like this and trace the
repercussions. For example, suppose the EEC policy is to pay subsidies to
European farmers to grow sugar beet. A good year produces a glut. The
price of sugar beet falls. European producers are sheltered by subsidies,
but Jamaican cane sugar growers are not and are badly hit by a fall in
sugar prices. They are further hit by the EEC policy of shedding its

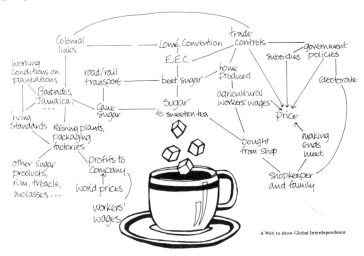

A Web to show Global Interdependence

surpluses of beet sugar through food aid to Third World countries. Sugar
cane is not Jamaica's only export but it is an important one so this change
in the world market has severe economic repercussions for it. Since
Jamaica is also politically unstable it may have political repercussions,
too. In other words, it is not enough to illustrate connections, it is
necessary also to demonstrate the dynamics of the system.

Some of the approaches suggested for conveying the political and
economic implications of Third World issues would apply here also.
However, to get pupils used to the notion of systems it is advisable to look
at some which are more concrete and more familiar. They may have
already looked at the ecological system in other lessons. If so, it would be
worth reminding them of this. Another possibility is to take a local issue
and relate it to local, regional, national and international factors. For
instance, why is a local school to be closed; (falling rolls, ageing local

population, cuts in local government expenditure, government's economic policy, etc.); or why is a local factory to be closed? (recession, rationalization of the industry, loss of markets to more competitive firms, etc.).

Handling controversy

In Chapter One it was pointed out that in deciding how to treat controversial subject matter in the classroom (whether, for example, to adopt a balanced, neutral or committed approach), it is necessary to take into account the knowledge, experience, prejudices and opinions pupils bring into the classroom with them. So, for example, there is a case for adopting the role of devil's advocate when confronted by a class full of youngsters who all voice the same unquestioning prejudice.

Nevertheless, compared with some of the other issues in this book, it is probable that pupils are unlikely to be as well informed or to have such strong preconceived opinions about many Third World issues. In such circumstances 'selling a particular line' can be mis-educative. It would be preferable to concentrate on helping pupils to develop a more critical, questioning approach in which no document, film or mass media account is taken for granted, and in which they subject their own and other people's opinions (including those of their teachers) to critical examination.

The key to helping pupils to develop a questioning approach is to decide what sorts of questions they should be encouraged to ask. I will conclude therefore by suggesting a few questions which need to be asked when considering public statements from the North and the South on Third World issues. The list is by no means comprehensive, but I hope will serve to provoke further thought about the nature of a questioning approach.

Concerning any official statement, article, newspaper editorial, film commentary or personal statement about a Third World country or issue:

  –What does it say about the causes of the situation or issue?
  –Does it raise the issue of responsibility?
  –What information (historical, economic or political) has been or appears to have been omitted from this account?
  –What motives can you think of which might account for such omissions?
  –Are certain points emphasized and others played down?
  –What solutions to the problem or issue are proposed (if any)?
  –Are there any other solutions which have been overlooked?
  –What reasons can you think of which might account for these other solutions being left out?
  –What attempt is made, if any, to see the issue from a Third World perspective?

6

Nuclear weapons

Bridget Baines and Michael Noctor

In 1974 UNESCO recommended that all students should study 'the maintenance of peace, types of war, disarmament'. This was repeated and expanded in 1979 and 1980 (**1**). The development of a new generation of nuclear weapons towards the end of the 1970s led to growing public concern and an expansion of the peace movement. The resultant burgeoning of interest in schools has been such that, according to Rick Rodgers, '. . . peace education has quietly become a widely respected and widely taught school and college subject in the UK' (**2**). These developments have gained support at higher and further education levels, and within local authorities and teacher unions. Several organizations such as Teachers for Peace and the Peace Education Network provide resources and support for teachers.

However, such developments have not been received with equanimity by some politicians and sections of the media. Anxiety has been aroused first because of party political divisions, and second, on account of the received view of what is actually taking place in schools, with misconceptions about the intentions of teachers who deal with nuclear weapons as an issue. In fact, the situation is not as clearcut as is sometimes assumed; facile reactions to the teaching of this issue often stem from assumptions about teachers' objectives and strategies which are outdated and inappropriate. In addition, the powers of the local education authority are under fresh scrutiny; for example, recommendations are misconstrued by some as edicts, and the ability of local education committees to intervene in any one school's curriculum is also under question (**3**). This amalgam of pressures from outside the school system renders the issue politically sensitive in a different way from the other issues in this book.

Why teach it?

In spite of some pressure, many schools choose to include the study of the nuclear arms situation in a range of different courses. The arguments for doing so include:

i) *The intrinsic importance of the issue.* In school courses reliant on current affairs material it would be difficult to exclude an issue so widely discussed in the media and by the general populace. As pupils are not isolated from the rest of society such issues understandably concern them.

ii) *The need to equip young people for participation in adult life and citizenship.* As an issue of national and international importance, some knowledge of the complexities of the issue is seen as a necessity.

iii) *A concern for the alarming nature of the issue.* Because of the prevalence of the issue in the media, much of which assumes some level of knowledge and views on nuclear weapons, some pupils may become anxious. While this is seen by certain people as an argument for not teaching about the issue, others think that much of the fear springs from ignorance and a sense of helplessness which may be at least partially dispelled by open discussion.

iv) *The use of the issue as a case study.* Because the issue is both controversial and currently under wide discussion it offers a useful case study of how the media present an issue, the work of pressure groups, the use of propaganda and so on.

Controversy within the issue
The levels of controversy about most aspects of the issue of nuclear arms render it both difficult and rewarding as a classroom topic. Many questions can be raised to which a range of often contradictory answers might be explored, such answers posing potential dilemmas of thought and action. A number of these questions are set out in the chart opposite.

At various points in these discussions, historical factors may be brought in. Indeed, some hold the view that a knowledge of the historical contexts is essential. Study of these contexts usually includes:

–Hiroshima (and to a lesser extent, Nagasaki); the events (over which there is some controversy) leading up to the dropping of the two bombs;
–the Cold War;
–historical concepts of nuclear war and deterrence, such as the 'balance of power', Mutually Assured Destruction, 'theatre war', etc.;
–the new situation (there is some disagreement as to whether there *is* one);
–SALT and START talks and Test Ban Treaties.

Problems and constraints

These may be extrinsic or intrinsic to the issue, and whether they are major or minor constraints can depend on school situation, type of course, age and ability of pupils.

What is at issue?

The weaponry:	Which of the two superpowers (the USA and the USSR) is superior in terms of nuclear capability?
	How should this capability be judged – which countries' weapons should be counted or ignored?
	Are Cruise missiles intended as first-strike weapons or not?
Deterrence:	Has the existence of nuclear weapons ensured peace? Will it do so in the future?
	Does the siting of Cruise missiles in this country increase or decrease the likelihood of nuclear war?
	Does the increasing sophistication and accuracy of nuclear weaponry make nuclear war more or less likely?
	Are British weapons a deterrent on their own or only in combination with NATO/European weaponry?
	Does a balance of numbers of missiles or warheads need to be maintained for deterrence, even if this includes a high overkill capacity?
	Is extended Civil Defence a necessity for a credible policy of deterrence?
Britain and international relations:	Should American weapons be based in this country? If so, who should control their use?
	How do relationships over nuclear weapons affect the development and use of conventional weapons?
	What is Britain's relationship to the rest of Europe in terms of a) further build-up of arms; b) multilateral or unilateral disarmament?
	Does the Soviet Union pose a threat to a) Western Europe; b) America?
	Is peace the absence of war or a state qualitatively different?
Future possibilities:	In a nuclear war, can there be a winner?
	Is a nuclear war being planned for?
	Would current planning for Civil Defence provide adequate protection in the event of nuclear war?
	Is disarmament possible?
	What might happen if Britain disarmed unilaterally?
	Could multilateral disarmament be achieved, and how?
	Is it better to be 'red than dead', and are these the only possibilities?
Moral arguments:	Are nuclear weapons morally justifiable?
	Do possible effects on the ecology and biosphere add an additional moral element to the arguments or not?
	Are the moral and philosophical grounds for or against using nuclear weapons the same as those associated with 'conventional' warfare?

External problems

1 *Political sensitivity* This has already been referred to briefly. Dealing with the issue may be seen by some as subversive in itself. It has been suggested that those teachers who are prepared to discuss the issue at all are likely to be CND supporters and therefore suspect as having a biased, even polemical line which, it is assumed, will lead to indoctrination. The Secretary of State for Education, Sir Keith Joseph, has been reported as wanting to keep nuclear issues out of examinations (**4**); Norman Tebbit, MP recommended parents in his constituency to keep children at home rather than allow attendance at plays that deal with peace issues put on in schools (**5**). The *Sun* summed up this view in an editorial as '. . . trying to turn innocent vulnerable youngsters into tools of propaganda' (**6**). These views are based on the notion of pupils as *tabulae rasae* and the assumption that teachers will rely on the transmission mode of teaching.

Although these claims have an inhibiting effect on teachers and schools, there seems to be little substance to them, as the following report suggests:

Peace bias claim denied

TEACHERS of peace studies cannot be accused of indoctrinating pupils or of teaching "appeasement studies", according to a survey commissioned by the British Atlantic Committee, the educational arm of the North Atlantic Treaty Organisation.

Mr Colin Gordon, lecturer specialising in West European defence at Salford University, who conducted the three-month survey, commented this week: "I was extremely impressed with the way in which teachers of peace studies take care to be as unbiased as possible. I found that they are not deliberately trying to impress controversial views. They are, in fact, presenting a good balance of views."

His findings are likely to come as an acute embarrassment to both the British Atlantic Committee and the Government which have vociferously condemned peace studies as overtly biased in favour of unilateralism and "appeasement".

The BAC's education committee is currently considering the findings which come in an interim report. It is planned to present the final report to a meeting, organised in association with Nottinghamshire education authority, in Nottingham on March 23.

Mr Ken Aldred, director of operations at BAC, said that despite Mr Gordon's findings he was still afraid that teachers of peace studies were biased in their teaching in favour of unilateralism.

He said: "I am very concerned that students of peace studies should take into account the whole range of views on ways of bringing about peace. I have my fears that this is not always being done."

But Mr Geoff Foster, chairman of the National Union of Teachers' international relations committee, said he was delighted with Mr Gordon's findings.

"They totally vindicate all that the Union has been saying about peace studies. Of course teachers are presenting a balanced view on the nuclear issue. We have always rejected allegations that peace studies teachers are engaged in indoctrination."

Amongst the courses and materials examined by Mr Gordon were the Atlantic College two-year peace studies course, the Avon Peace Project, a three-year venture funded by the Rowntree Trust to develop peace studies materials, run workshops for teachers and promote peace projects in schools, the World Studies Teacher Training Centre at York University, and the teaching resource, *The Nuclear Question—an issue to debate*, produced by Tressell Publications.　　*The Teacher* 25.2.83

2 *Limitations of resources* Many teachers who deal with the question of nuclear weapons do not have access to a wide range of tried and trusted resources. The recent upsurge of activity and concern has been fragmented in nature, and some teachers have had to create their own materials in order to present the wide range of information and views which they consider desirable. (The bibliography for this chapter provides details of some resources available.)

3 *Developmental constraints* Considerable demands may be made on pupils' ability to conceptualize, hypothesize and retain several conflicting ideas simultaneously. Teaching methods may have to take developmental levels of pupils into account, with more emphasis on a skills-based approach. This might be less of a constraint when dealing with concepts which have wider connotations and are familiar to pupils, such as different forms of conflict, interdependence of nations, etc.

Internal problems

1 *Complexity* The issue is complex and involves considerations of

    a)   technical aspects of nuclear weapons such as the nature of delivery systems and the consequences of explosions both immediate and long term;

    b)   various military strategies and scenarios;

    c)   international relations;

    d)   the historical development of the arms race;

    e)   the range of different arguments and options concerning nuclear weapons.

If one's aim is that the pupils should acquire some understanding of the issue rather than using it as a case study, then a considerable amount of work is required to explore it. One head of a social studies department said: 'The ultimate aim of the course is that they should be aware of the major policy alternatives and . . . work out a stance for themselves . . . but the complexity of the arguments are way over the heads of quite a lot of them. The problem is that simplifying it doesn't do justice to the argument.'

2 *Fear and anxiety in pupils* The prospect of a nuclear war is horrific. It is not surprising that many people feel that this issue is just too frightening for school children to deal with. Recent studies carried out in both America and the Netherlands suggest that children are deeply disturbed by the threat of nuclear war. Many consider that it is inevitable (**7**). The teacher quoted earlier also said, 'Most of them feel that nuclear war is possible and most of them feel that if it happens they're dead and what's the point of doing much about it? But they also feel they're so distanced from the decision-making machinery that what they feel is of marginal importance.'

For those who see these as arguments in support of teaching the issue, these possible reactions are nevertheless a constraint. Some teachers seek to dissipate anxiety and helplessness by including discussion of the positive activities of pressure groups such as Greenham Common Peace Camp, CND, END, Women for Defence, the British Atlantic Committee, and discussion of individual action such as writing to MPs.

3 *Nuclear weapons and international relations* If pupils display mistrust and ignorance of other nationalities and countries (as many do), open and critical considerations of various aspects of the nuclear arms debate will be hampered. Again, wider concepts previously encountered and developed when teaching other topics may help.

4 *Polarization* Because of the many contradictions and complexities of this issue, often falling too easily into opposition, there is a strong possibility of the arguments polarizing (for and against, USA v. USSR, unilateral v. multilateral disarmament, etc.). This may be compounded by the developmental difficulties already mentioned. Yet polarization can render the arguments simplistic, although more apparently comprehensible.

The role of the teacher

Disagreements over the teacher's role when introducing material about nuclear arms to pupils focus on the role of the teacher and his or her personal views. As already noted, assumptions are sometimes made that transmission modes of teaching are used to convey a one-sided view to pupils. However, many teachers consider such teacher-dominated approaches to be inappropriate for most controversial issues, excluding as they would do the views of pupils and the central nature and purpose of studying such issues in school.

Robin Richardson (**8**) advocates greater participation and equality in the classroom as being necessary in dealing with controversial issues, as pupils learn experientially from the form of the lessons as well as from the lesson content: '. . . this style of teaching involves providing students with the space and the security which they need if they are to face uncomfortable and painful challenges, specifically the challenge of *unlearning*—that is, realizing that much of their current knowledge is not knowledge at all, but misinformation and prejudice.'

The complex information to be considered, the different viewpoints to be discussed and the variety of materials and activities (which will be discussed in a later section), require open responses and teaching methods that initiate and facilitate such responses. It is also not seen as an issue where pupils will have 'answers' or 'conclusions' but rather one where views may develop and more information be assimilated over a period of time. The fact that the issue is controversial outside the classroom increases the likelihood of radically differing views inside the classroom;

pupils cannot therefore be thought of as a homogeneous group committed to a single consensus view.

Similarly, teachers will have widely differing views on this as on other subjects, and most older pupils are aware of this diversity. Many teachers feel that in the course of classroom discussion, when trying to create a climate where views are both readily expressed and listened to, it is proper for them to express their views, especially if asked. They feel it is important that pupils see they have some views, albeit individual and open to further discussion or even criticism. Far from transmitting conscious bias, this helps pupils perceive it, enabling them to make judgements in the light of it.

A number of teachers, arguing that 'balanced teaching' and 'balanced learning' are very different (see Chapter One), feel that it is important to counter the often one-sided information that pupils already receive and help them perceive a range of possibilities. One teacher put it like this:

> We see *The War Game*, and of course that is biased in a particular direction, but I feel that by the time the pupils come to see the film they have an adequate amount of opposing ideas coming from the media and I think the film plays a role in redressing an imbalance that is created by the media in that respect.

Course contexts

Unlike the issue of sexism, nuclear arms is usually seen more as a discrete topic, although some advocates of peace studies regard it as bound up with issues of power and the use of violence throughout society. The course within which it appears and whether it is to be treated either as a case study or in its own right will be important in dictating approaches. The process-based approach that aims at teaching concepts usually involves the exploration of different contexts and applications, through which the concepts may be expanded, generalized and tested. This issue may be used to study the nature of conflict, forms of international co-operation, the preoccupation of nation states with their international standing (highlighted perhaps by the development of nuclear weapons by Third World countries), and so on. This spiral of concepts and applications is a particular feature of peace studies. Some English courses might use the issue in a similar way, perhaps as part of a module on the language of persuasion or politics, literature about war, or protest poetry.

Where the issue of nuclear arms is used as a topic of interest or concern in its own right, the concepts developed or expounded in the rest of the course may still provide a background for discussions. In a political education course, for example, earlier study of pressure groups and national government might provide an entry point and context for discussion of partisan materials on nuclear issues.

The course context will contribute answers to questions such as:

-What knowledge is essential? (scientific, political, historical)
-Should we be teaching skills, and what sort? (For example, Pax Christi's Peace Education programme emphasizes conflict resolution.)
-What values form the basis of the work on this issue? (Unlike some other issues, such as racism or sexism, there is no liberal consensus or legislation to point to.)

In addition, questions of method will be influenced by teaching styles current on the course as well as the nature of the issue. Robin Richardson's observations earlier in the chapter would be apposite here, as would his views on the desirability of building a classroom climate appropriate to teaching all such issues (**8**).

The chart below shows the outline of a five-day project carried out in a Netherlands comprehensive school (**7**). It shows a range of teaching methods and learning activities, and a combination of cognitive and skills-based teaching. While such an intensive project is unusual (though not unheard of) in this country, the elements in it may be adapted for use in a more usual type of course.

Project structure

Day	Theme	Main activity	Object
1	Weapons in the Netherlands	Visit to barracks	Pupils experience the presence of weapons in the Netherlands.
2	Why armaments?	Playing of a simulation game	Pupils gain insight into arguments for armament and disarmament.
3	A new situation: nuclear weapons	Watching a tape about nuclear weapons and a discussion on opinions about nuclear weapons	Pupils gain insight into a new situation which has arisen through the introduction of nuclear weapons and are forming an opinion about that.
4	Is disarmament possible?	Visit to action groups	Pupils gain insight into the possibilities with regard to disarmament.
5	Present own opinion with regard to armaments and disarmament	Painting, writing, making own tape	Pupils are giving information on the subject to others.

Learning activities

We have described below some of the various activities used by teachers when dealing with the issue of nuclear weapons. This is by no means a comprehensive list of teaching methods and we have not dealt with more traditional approaches, feeling that teachers have ample experience of these. Instead we have chosen to describe some of the diverse methods increasingly being used by teachers when handling controversy. Our view is that a combination of approaches is the most interesting and effective way of handling this issue. Choices over which methods are most appropriate and decisions concerning structuring of courses and units, are necessarily made on the basis of local circumstances.

Pupils' views

> *We wouldn't be afraid of Russia if we knew any Russians. Probably they're just like us.*

> *There will never be any going back from the bomb. There will always be the suspicion that someone else has one hidden away, or that they could build one. Countries will all get secret ones then.*

These views were expressed by two fourth-year secondary school pupils after a lesson about the nuclear weapons issue. These two views represent quite distinct perspectives: the first is a view often held by unilateralists; the second is one that some retentionists would agree with. There are a number of reasons for enabling pupils to express their opinions, feelings and views when dealing with the issue of nuclear weapons. In particular, where a divergence of opinion exists, such an exercise may prove a useful way into the issue by providing the basis of the different perspectives concerning the maintenance of nuclear weapons. These perspectives can then be explored further using a variety of other methods. Also, most fourth- and fifth-year pupils will have some knowledge of the issue and some will be well informed. An advantage of this approach is that it provides the teacher with some idea of the needs of the group enabling him/her to devise further activities and to select resources that take pupils' attitudes and knowledge into account. In this sense this exercise could be a diagnostic one giving an indication of whether pupils are upset or disturbed by the issue; the extent to which they lack essential knowledge; the bases from which pupils are arguing (e.g. 'aggression is natural' or 'violence is inherently immoral').

Eliciting pupils' views can be done in a number of ways. Deciding whether to start by having pupils express their views publicly—either through conducting an open 'opinionnaire' or allowing these to emerge in small group discussion—or requiring pupils to make individual written responses which can then be collated by the teacher, will depend on the area in which the teaching takes place and the character of the particular group of pupils. One useful starting-point for this approach is to ask pupils to write down what comes to mind when they think of, for example,

Russia, America, the arms race, nuclear weapons, etc. This approach could be developed along the lines of the 'mental map' described in Chapter Five.

As one way of introducing the issue of nuclear arms this approach has much to commend it, provided that the way in which the views are aired does not inhibit those who hold a minority view from expressing it, or result in a competitive polarization which may have the effect of entrenching the views that are held. Where such a danger exists it may be that engaging pupils in individually written responses avoids these problems while providing the teacher with a very useful form of diagnostic assessment.

By contrast, small group discussion may provide a means of enabling the majority of pupils to express their points of view without undue inhibition. Our experience with the use of small groups for this purpose has been encouraging. Once groups are carefully selected to avoid personality clashes, far more constructive discussions can take place providing pupils with the opportunity to work through their ideas.

Engaging the whole class in discussion, on the other hand, provides the teacher with the opportunity of taking account of all the views that are expressed while allowing the individual pupil's ideas to develop more. It does seem likely, however, that an all-class discussion of the issue might prove more fruitful once pupils have had a chance to consider and reflect on the various aspects of the issue. Early discussions may 'fix' pupils' ideas so that the subsequent material may be less likely to be treated in an open, critical and unprejudiced manner.

Use of visitors

On some issues it may be difficult to use outside speakers who represent the whole range of views held on the issue (for example in the case of Northern Ireland). Nuclear weapons, however, is a topic that can more easily benefit from their use. There are a number of organizations whose members visit schools and do so largely without creating any adverse political reaction. The approaches used by these groups are diverse: lectures, discussion, showing film/slide shows, running role plays or drama workshops, presenting plays. One of the commonest complaints heard about outsiders who come into schools for work with pupils is the tendency to pitch the level too high as a result of inexperience or through lack of knowledge of the pupils and school. Despite the variation in the quality of performance and the undoubted problems of getting the level right, there are a number of positive advantages.

When these visitors represent pressure groups such as the British Atlantic Committee (which is government-funded and promotes NATO and the policy of nuclear deterrence) or the Campaign for Nuclear Disarmament, or Schools Against the Bomb (both of whom campaign for unilateral nuclear disarmament), they often have a very detailed knowledge of various aspects of the issue which the teacher may lack. Often simply because they provide new faces or because they employ a novel approach the lesson is enlivened by their presence. This may be further enhanced because they are actively involved in the issue and consequently lend an air of reality to it.

When several such speakers are introduced a range of different inter-pretations, opinions and policies can be presented by those who hold them, thus avoiding the difficulty for the teacher of presenting the range of positions without caricaturing them.

It is not always possible when engaging visitors to be fully aware in advance of their particular point of view and the extent of their skills when dealing with school pupils. Attempts at 'balancing' speakers against each other in terms of what they are presenting are not straightforward. Even if they address the same questions and issues, have equal time, and the presentations appear to balance each other, extraneous factors such as the charisma of the speakers or their status means that it is impossible to make assumptions about balance simply by having opposing speakers.

Pupils are often sceptical of committed speakers and many operate very selectively when listening to them. Having attended a session by some peace activists at the school, one fourth-year pupil commented:

> They are very brave to do what they did. They believe in it but I think that might put people off. It's like assembly where you don't listen just because you know the people believe in it strongly.

Whatever types of speaker or group are brought in from outside, the onus is still on the classroom teacher to help pupils to consider these viewpoints in the light of their own opinions to deal with questions pupils may pose and to allow space for assimilation. Coordination and planning for all these features is no mean task, and may limit opportunities for 'ad hoc' forms of teaching which are often appropriate to other topics, especially in current affairs.

For and against approaches

The nature of disputes can often be highlighted by examining and contrasting opposing views. At its best this process can be a particularly useful way both of exploring the issue in a comparative framework and of developing pupils' critical thinking. However, there is a need to avoid oversimplifying the disputes into two caricatured perspectives, when they are often multifaceted issues over which there is a range of competing views.

There are a number of ways that the for and against technique can be used including identifying the strengths and weaknesses of arguments or statements and developing arguments in favour of, and against, certain policies and options. One way of involving pupils in this approach would be through an enquiry exercise which would engage pairs or small groups in identifying the different viewpoints from a range of resources. These resources could usefully include books which outline the various arguments concerning the issue, such as the *Nuclear Weapons and Warfare* collection (**9**), *A Question to Debate: The Nuclear Issue* (**10**) or *Nuclear Issues* (**11**), as well as partisan material from the Ministry of Defence or from CND.

The 'nuclear weapons issue' really consists of a number of related issues and so it is best when adopting this approach to focus on one aspect, encouraging pupils to be as comprehensive as possible when listing the various viewpoints in relation to this.

The section 'What is at issue' on p. 91 outlines a number of contentious questions about nuclear weapons, some of which could provide starting-points for this exercise.

Here is an example of how some of these arguments might be listed.

Do nuclear weapons prevent attack?

YES	NO
Nuclear weapons provide the capability of inflicting immense damage on an aggressor to the extent that this would outweigh any possible advantage.	Our Nuclear weapons do not present a credible threat. If they were ever used by this country the result would be its total annihilation.
Throughout history peace has been maintained by a balance of force. Nuclear weapons have maintained East–West peace for the past 40 years.	The balance of terror contributes to an atmosphere of insecurity and thus increases the likelihood of a nuclear holocaust as the result of a panic attack.

Source: Adapted from **9**.

Simulations and role-play

Many simulations and role-plays are used with this issue and are designed to provide insight and understanding of different aspects such as the escalation of the arms race, the pressures under which governments and various interest groups operate, and the sorts of considerations which they take into account when making decisions. Some are designed, for example, to show what it would feel like to be inside a fall-out shelter or to be a survivor of a nuclear holocaust, while others focus on a local dispute to provide a starting point for raising wider issues. Some of these approaches are outlined opposite.

The disarmament dilemma

This employs two sides, one representing the USA, the other the USSR, and is played over 20 rounds. At the start the USA has 95 points and the USSR 88 points. Each side has to make decisions as to whether to arm or disarm at each round, for which they are then awarded points on the basis of: if one side disarms and the other arms the disarmers are awarded −5 points, the armers +5; if both disarm, then both are awarded −3 points; and if both arm they are awarded +3 points each. Three further factors complicate the game. i) If one side obtains a 50-point lead, it achieves first strike capability and can attack if and when it chooses—if it does so the game is over. ii) Should either side acquire 120 points or more (representing a very large nuclear arsenal), then the risk of accident is considered to be high and a dice is thrown. If the throw is a six, this results in a nuclear holocaust. iii) The controller can introduce a number of other factors such as civil unrest or tension in one of the world's flashpoints. The source for this game is *The Nuclear Arms Race II: Proliferation and Disarmament* (**9**)

Role-plays involving various interest groups, the arms trade and the arms race

There are a number of these games available, for instance, the *Arms Trade Game* (**12**), *Finger on the Button* (**13**) and a simulation included in the UNICEF school series No. 6 *An approach to peace education* pack (**14**). The basic principle of these games is that students act out the roles of different people or groups of people who are involved in the issue. So, for example, *Finger on the Button* involves the participants in acting out the roles of members of the British Cabinet considering defence policy and spending; the UNICEF game includes representatives of the military, scientists, civilians opposed to nuclear weapons, diplomats, industrial workers, etc.; whereas the *Arms Trade Game* involves arms makers, arms sellers and arms buyers. Another approach would be to create a fictional public enquiry to which various local groups have to present their case concerning the siting of nuclear weapons in a locality. As no public enquiry has so far taken place in real life, this is a very hypothetical exercise. Nevertheless, it sets the problem of mustering several different lines of argument for consideration.

Such exercises as these are time-consuming and consequently require some thought in planning and execution if they are to be successful. A distinctive feature of role-plays and simulations is that the learning experiences vary to some extent according to the different roles that are enacted by each pupil. These different experiences need to be 'pooled' in order to capitalize fully on the exercise, and it is for this reason that a reflective element needs to be built into the process. This often takes the form of a 'feedback' session once the exercise is complete—although in many cases it is useful to interject at certain points in order to focus attention on an aspect which is of general importance at the time.

Simulations and role-plays have gained considerable popularity. The growth of peace education and its emphasis on the importance of the process of learning means that there is a growing body of resources and methods available which employ experiential learning and focus on the nuclear issue. Advocates of such exercises feel they provide powerful learning experiences although the nature of this learning is inherently difficult to assess. However, they are enjoyable when used as part of a module or unit on nuclear war and seem to be usefully employed mid-way through dealing with this issue for two reasons. First there is often a low point at this stage, when enthusiasm sags and role-plays and simulations are usually effective motivators. Second, for the exercise to be useful some background work is necessary (the nature of this depends on the focus of the course and the type of game being used), and the insights gained can then be usefully built upon.

Literature

Different types of literature, such as fiction, poetry, drama and eye-witness accounts, are sometimes used to stimulate thought on this issue. The grounds for doing so are that these introduce affective and experiential angles which may deepen appreciation of the possible outcome of nuclear war. Technological information often omits or obscures these aspects of the issue. The mere figures fail to convey consequences at an individual level, and instead often encourage the glib or facile response.

Encouraging pupils' own written responses to both fictitious and factual material also requires the empathetic, imaginative, affective skills drawn upon by literature. Several useful suggestions here are given in *Nuclear Issues*, by Nikki Haydon and Jim Mulligan (**11**). Plays for performance, poetry or imaginative writing accompanied by pictures for a wall display or project will all involve pupils actively and creatively.

Conclusion

Most of the materials dealing with this issue are partisan, and judging them and using them requires familiarity with a range of different points of view, historical background, technological and political factors. For teachers and pupils, the need for critical thinking, the building of knowledge and analytical concepts are paramount. In the light of these requirements, a prerequisite of any series of sessions would be a generous allocation of time and a planned variety of activity.

7

An overview

Robert Stradling, Michael Noctor and Bridget Baines

To attempt to make generalizations about any aspect of teaching, let alone the teaching of controversial issues, calls for either a thick skin or latent masochistic tendencies. For every teacher willing to acknowledge that his or her experiences in the classroom parallel the researcher's observations there will be another who rejects them out of hand. Given the wide variations to be found in school curricula and practices that is hardly surprising. However, a number of common problems and themes have emerged in the preceding chapters and we feel that in this final chapter it would be worth while exploring the possibility that common teaching problems call for common strategies and solutions. In doing this we shall also draw on some of the findings from research into the teaching of controversial issues which we and other curriculum researchers and evaluators have conducted in recent years.

Our research was conducted in 1981–83 and involved extensive classroom observation in 20 schools distributed throughout the North East, South West and South East of England. In 1981 we also sent out a questionnaire to a national sample of schools to obtain information about the kinds of controversial issues being taught in schools, the contexts in which they appeared, the constraints operating in schools which affect choice of issues and teaching methods, and the problems encountered in the classroom.

Selecting issues

In recent years the GCE and CSE Examination Boards have increasingly included controversial issues in their syllabuses for social studies, humanities, history, geography, civics and politics. So for some teachers the question of which issues to choose does not arise. They teach controversial issues because the syllabus requires it. For the rest this remains a significant question. In our survey of schools we found that the ten controversial issues listed below are the ones which are most widely taught to young people in the 14–16 age range.

Other issues widely taught and also considered highly controversial include minority rights (e.g. the treatment of gypsies), environmental issues (conservation, pollution, energy resources, etc.), industrial relations, and the role of the police in the community.

The top ten controversial issues in schools

1   Crime and Punishment
2   Nuclear Weapons and Disarmament
3   Sexuality
4   Race Relations and Racial Discrimination
5   Health Issues (drug abuse, glue sniffing, alcoholism, smoking, etc.)
6   Unemployment and Poverty
7   Moral Issues (e.g. abortion, euthanasia, etc.)
8   Third World and North–South Relations
9   Northern Ireland
10   Sexism and Sexual Discrimination

However, perhaps it is more revealing to examine the issues which many schools still shy away from. The range of 'untouchable issues' is fairly narrow. The rights, treatment and social acceptability of certain sexual minorities (homosexuals and lesbians) and some sexual practices such as paedophilia and incest are frequently mentioned by headteachers and heads of departments as being too politically sensitive to be introduced into courses for the young school leaver. We also found that a number of teachers, whilst willing to discuss school issues (corporal punishment, strikes and other forms of direct action by teachers, etc.), would do so in only a general, abstract way. They were not prepared to discuss specific instances or the positions adopted by personalities involved. Once again it tends to be the political sensitivity of the issues within the local community rather than the controversial nature of the issue within society at large which appears to be the strongest inhibiting factor.

It is now a commonly held view within the teaching profession that the interest of the pupils is most likely to be aroused by topics which they perceive to be relevant to their everyday lives. Some years ago one of the authors conducted a study of the political education of young school leavers and found that while many of them claimed that politics was 'boring', 'pointless', 'nothing to do with us', they were interested in political issues, often not associating such issues with the world of politics as portrayed by the mass media and politicians themselves (1). Their interest in issues can often range widely: from unemployment to mugging; from the threat of nuclear war to the provision of better recreational facilities for young people; from the restoration of capital punishment in our courts to the abolition of corporal punishment in our schools.

Many teachers have responded to the challenge by developing units of lessons based on issues which clearly affect pupils' lives or will affect their lives in the foreseeable future. As researchers we have seen numerous highly successful examples of this kind of approach but it is necessary to bear in mind that the teacher's view of what is likely to be relevant and interesting to pupils does not always coincide with the pupils' own perceptions. Again, one of the authors can recall sitting in on a general studies lesson in a South London further education college. All the students were West Indian and the lecturer raised the issue of the 'Sus Law' for group discussion. This was at a time when the picking up of young West Indians on suspicion by the police was a highly controversial issue within the local community. To the observer—and to the lecturer—this seemed the ideal issue for classroom discussion and yet the students were clearly reluctant to get involved. When asked why they did not want to discuss this issue they replied that they had to live with this kind of thing every day of the week. Inside the college they wanted something different.

We raise this point not as a direct criticism of all those teachers who try to make their teaching 'more relevant'. We do so simply to point out that there is a good case for involving pupils in the whole process of selecting issues either by having a general discussion at the beginning of term regarding the topics to be dealt with, or by giving pupils a questionnaire to find out which issues interest them the most, or by having sufficient flexibility within the stucture of the course or unit to introduce issues when raised by pupils.

There is a second good reason why pupils should be involved in the selection of issues. Recent research by Eileen Wormald indicates that girls are often concerned about rather different controversial issues from boys. Where boys tend to focus on issues such as inflation, unemployment and war, girls are more likely to select issues such as homelessness, poverty and the number of people in the world who are starving (**2**).

Potential constraints

No doubt some readers may well be thinking by now that it is all very well our suggesting that pupils should be involved in the selection of issues but this does not take into account the kinds of constraints which operate in schools of their acquaintance. It is a fair point and might also apply to those curriculum developers and researchers who advocate the use of certain kinds of teaching methods when dealing with controversial subject matter. Thus, for example, Hamingson's evaluation of the Humanities Curriculum Project found that the mastery of the teacher's role as 'neutral chairman' involved a great deal of training and support, and considerable reorganization of classrooms and timetables was also necessary in many schools to create a climate conducive to extensive large group discussion (**3**). Increasingly curriculum researchers are arguing that teachers and other curriculum developers have to anticipate the kinds of internal and external constraints operating in schools before introducing a significant innovation in curriculum content, aims or methods.

Four main categories of constraint on the teaching of controversial issues operated in most of the schools we were associated with:

1 *Teacher constraints* E.g. lack of knowledge about highly complex, contemporary issues; the teacher's perception of the aims, content and methods of their 'subject' or academic discipline; teachers' perceptions of what is and is not 'acceptable' as subject matter for teaching; and the teachers' personalities.

2 *School constraints*
a) Constraints arising out of the structure and organization of the school, e.g. timetabling arrangements; the hidden curriculum; classroom design; potential disapproval of the head; potential disapproval of colleagues; the prevailing climate within the school regarding the status of your course and the methods you adopt.
b) Constraints operating within the classroom, e.g. pupils' beliefs and prejudices; pupils' expectations regarding the purpose and content of the course; pupils' lack of familiarity with the kinds of teaching methods you are using.

3 *External constraints* E.g. fear of disapproval by parents, board of management or school governors, local education committee, or influential local interests.

4 *Issue-specific constraints* That is, constraints inherent in the teaching of an issue:
a) Constraints raised by a specific issue. We have discussed a number of these in previous chapters. For instance, teaching about sexism (or combating it in schools) faces different constraints in all-boys' schools compared with all-girls' schools, or even coeducational schools.
b) Constraints imposed on the teacher by virtually any controversial issue; e.g. with contemporary controversial issues we do not have the benefit of hindsight regarding the significance of recent events, the issue is not yet resolved, the outcome may be unpredictable; the teacher is intervening in a learning process which has already begun outside the classroom and is being reinforced at home and by the mass media; the primary sources of evidence or information which one would have to use are likely to be incomplete, biased and contradictory; and it may still be difficult to establish criteria for determining what does and does not constitute valid evidence or information. By way of illustration of this point, the reader might care to consider the significance of these constraints in teaching about an issue like Northern Ireland, the Falkland Islands war, or nuclear disarmament.

Of the 'teacher constraints' listed above perhaps the two most frequent, persistent and problematic are personality factors and teachers' perceptions of the nature of their subject. So, for example, the reactions of a number of teachers to the prospect of adopting the role of 'neutral chairman' was to say that they did not feel their personalities were well suited to such a role either because they felt too committed to be impartial or, more frequently, because they felt uneasy about open-ended discussion which they could not control or direct. It is tempting to respond to such reactions with well-meaning platitudes: 'Horses for courses' or 'There's more than one way to skin a cat!' seem appropriate responses on such occasions. However, whilst such reactions might well apply to the use of a specific method such as 'procedural neutrality' or even 'open-ended discussion', they may be less appropriate when applied to the more general role of the teacher when teaching controversial issues. Because of the kinds of constraint listed in the 'Issue-specific' category, we believe that there is a strong case for teachers eschewing the role of 'expert' and opting instead to act as 'enablers'. That is, being able to provide appropriate learning experiences rather than expert knowledge of issues or, to put it another way, knowing the right questions to ask rather than the 'right answers'.

'School constraints' and 'Issue-specific constraints' have been a central concern of virtually every chapter in this book and so we will not dwell on them again at any length. The comments in Chapter Four on the effects of the hidden curriculum and the strategies suggested for circumventing such constraints might well apply to teaching a number of other issues. An equally significant constraint here can be the prevailing climate within the school towards the use of certain kinds of teaching methods and the pupils' lack of familiarity with them. Most of the teachers we have worked with in the last three years have tended to use a wide range of teaching methods when handling controversial issues—certainly a wider range than the methods commonly used by their colleagues in other subject areas. As a result they find that it often takes several weeks of small group discussion or 'procedural neutrality' or enquiry-based learning before pupils begin to feel familiar and at ease with such methods and start to respond in the way the teacher hoped.

The political sensitivity of some controversial issues and the consequent nervousness of some teachers and their heads regarding complaints from parents, governors and the local authority, as we pointed out earlier, is still seen as a major problem. The extract on p. 109 describes how one teacher set about deflecting potential criticisms both within and outside the school.

In Chapter One we promised or threatened a further word or two on indoctrination and this seems to be the appropriate point. Clearly, fear of indoctrination lies at the root of much of the public concern about teaching controversial issues, although the term indoctrination is often reserved only for attempts by teachers to engender support for values, attitudes and beliefs which are thought—for the time being—to be outside the assumed consensus. At present a great deal of health education appears to be concerned with changing pupils' attitudes towards smoking, use of drugs, alcohol and personal hygiene. Such attempts are seldom held to be iniquitous, unacceptable, or indoctrinatory.

In our research we have seen very few examples of indoctrination in the classical sense, i.e. a teacher with a doctrine or ideology which provides a coherent point of view on every issue and who teaches such points of view as if they were the only valid ones possible. Nevertheless, we have observed a number of teachers who adopt an explicit and consciously biased approach to some individual issues. Generally speaking, however, covert and implicit bias is far more widespread. It is apparent:

i)   in the implicit treatment of subject matter, e.g. some questions are picked up and elaborated on whilst others are ignored, some points are emphasized, others are not;

ii)   in the simplified and stereotyped treatment of points of view with which the teacher is unfamiliar or does not agree (e.g. 'All Conservatives are monetarists');

iii) in the selection and omission of topics (e.g. a lot of humanities teaching in the UK includes a unit of lessons on World War Two. It is often entitled 'Home Front' and children get the impression that all the aerial bombing was done by the Luftwaffe. There is seldom any reference to a German Home Front (or the occupation of Europe) or to the bombing of Dresden or Hamburg;

iv)   in the way in which teachers respond to the opinions, commitments and prejudices of their pupils.

One final point on bias and indoctrination. The overwhelming weight of research on the formation of social, political and religious attitudes and values indicates that factors outside the school are more influential. When teaching about controversial issues teachers are intervening in an already active learning process. By virtue of the fact that such issues are controversial it is likely that pupils will be exposed to alternative viewpoints and will recognize when they are being 'sold a line'. So, in a sense, teachers should neither hope to nor fear to influence pupils' attitudes to any significant degree. Indeed, indoctrination by default may be a cause for greater concern. For example, by avoiding certain issues, teachers may give pupils the idea that there is only one valid viewpoint on this issue—the one shared by their friends and family and by the culture or subculture in which they have been brought up. Certainly this is as good a way as any of preserving certain cultural stereotypes and ethnocentricities.

One school's approach to 'selling' a curriculum innovation

At a Faculty meeting held in early December, we moved hesitantly towards a plan of campaign. Our first task, as we saw it, was to anticipate as many objections as we could to our proposals for compulsory world studies. Each and every weakness in our case, seeming or real, had to be pinpointed and an answer—or answers—found. Likewise, each and every strength had to be drawn upon whilst bearing in mind how counterproductive it can be to sell a case to the point of overkill. We also needed allies. Accordingly, we decided from the outset to seek the support of influential figures within the catchment area; figures who would tend to reassure parents doubting the wisdom of our proposal by the very fact that they were seen to favour compulsory world studies. We were thinking of college governors, local councillors, local clergymen, and well-known and well-respected teachers working in local primary and high schools. Allies with particular expertise were also required: representatives from the worlds of business, industry and further and higher education, for example, who could speak with authority about the relevance of O/CSE world studies for the school leaver entering a career or taking his studies further.

Format for a meeting
Out of these initial ruminations emerged a format for the world studies consultation. The idea of a traditional-style parents' meeting, chaired from the dais, was discarded from the outset. Instead, we opted for a format which would more accurately reflect the ethos, as it was developing, of the world studies classroom and which would also facilitate in-depth consultation. The evening, we decided, should begin with a multi-media presentation outlining the aims and content of the world studies course, explaining the qualifications to which it would lead and seeking to anticipate likely queries about and objections to our proposals. The presentation, we felt, should be planned and executed by the entire teaching team. After the presentation, parents would be invited to repair to the humanities area to put their questions to and hear the points of view of people invited to sit on six panels or 'stalls'.

Advantages
The format seemed ideal for our purposes. It allowed for free-ranging and in-depth consultation. The use of stalls permitted a person-to-person exchange of views and reduced the likelihood of parents being too inhibited to speak as they so often are at a formal meeting chaired from the front. It was also an approach more likely to avoid the embattled positions so often evident at a formally run meeting where a participant, having made known his standpoint, is reluctant to lose face by shifting his position. A two-hour consultation allowed for a gradual shift of attitude as a result of a series of one-to-one conversations. The format was also a way of avoiding red herrings of an emotive nature. (How often have we seen a parents' meeting on the curriculum deflected from its original purpose by one or two dominant personalities ready to do battle about the credibility of CSE qualifications or about mixed-ability teaching!) Another consideration making the format an attractive proposition was that it permitted parents to put their questions to the person best able to answer them, which would not have been the case had all questions been fired at a world studies team facing the serried ranks of parents. Finally, the stalls were a useful device enabling us to demonstrate to parents that a number of prestigious local figures were prepared to give up an evening and give active support to our proposal.

Source: *New Era*, volume 60, 1979

Teaching strategies

For many teachers classroom discussion appears to be the main method. The following response from a head of religious education in a comprehensive school, is fairly typical:

> I tend to deal with controversial issues through discussion. I consider my role as teacher is to make sure that all aspects of the issue being talked about are brought out. I make it clear that what I say is as much open to criticism as anyone else in the group, and I go to great length to encourage criticism. I do not like to be in the position where a group accepts what I say without question. If they do I feel I've failed.

However, whilst other teachers use classroom discussion extensively, they also feel that it is necessary to ensure that discussion does not simply deteriorate into, as one head of remedial studies put it, 'slanging matches based on ignorance and blind prejudice as this serves only to reinforce shallow views'. Here discussion and debate is not the way in to looking at controversial issues but the finale of a series of lessons during which pupils have collected relevant information, watched films, listened to outside speakers, and used a variety of educational resources.

For some other teachers this enquiry-based approach is sufficient in itself. The lack of general discussion and airing of opinions, in their view, is more than compensated for by the acquisition of enquiry skills, a facility for asking relevant questions, and the opportunities which this approach affords for individual rather than group-paced learning.

One other general strategy is worth noting here. Some teachers in their responses to our questions emphasized the value of experiential learning when teaching about controversial issues. As one deputy head puts it:

> Give them problems to solve. Run a murder trial with defence and prosecution—get each juror to state reasons for his decision and the sentence. Give them local issues to discuss. Get them to take the side of a pressure group and present a case to local or national government. Involve them!

Another teacher points out that 'All issues manifest the conflicts in our society. Role play and simulation, and especially role reversal, give pupils the opportunity to step into the shoes of people actually affected by an issue and see things as they do.'

We also asked teachers about their opinions regarding some of the specific teaching methods such as neutral chairman or devil's advocate which have been proposed for handling controversial issues. Their perceptions of the strengths and weaknesses of these different methods are presented in the following chart. This consists of direct quotes from interviews and questionnaires. We have listed them under two headings:

'Potential strengths' and 'Potential weaknesses' since many of our respondents often prefaced their remarks with 'It all depends . . .'. We should also point out that the overwhelming majority of teachers felt that the ideal approach was somehow to combine the study of materials offering a balanced range of opinions on issues with open-ended discussion. For our own views on the problems of achieving a balance we refer the reader back to Chapter One.

Teachers' opinions on teaching strategies

Potential strengths	Procedural Neutrality	Potential weaknesses
Minimizes undue influence of teacher's own bias. Gives everyone a chance to take part in free discussion. Scope for open-ended discussion, i.e. the class may move on to consider issues and questions which the teacher hasn't thought of. Presents a good opportunity for pupils to exercise communication skills. Works well *if* you have a lot of background material.	In which the teacher adopts the role of an impartial chairperson of a discussion group.	Pupils find it artificial. Can damage the rapport between teacher and class if it doesn't work. Depends on pupils being familiar with the method elsewhere in the school or it will take a long time to acclimatize them. May only reinforce pupils' existing attitudes and prejudices. Very difficult with the less able. *Neutral chair* doesn't suit my personality.
Pupils will try to guess what the teacher thinks anyway. Stating your own position makes everything above board. If pupils know where the teacher stands on the issue they can discount his or her prejudices and biases. It's better to state your preferences *after* discussion rather than before. It should only be used if pupils' dissenting opinions are treated with respect. It can be an excellent way of maintaining credibility with pupils since they do not expect us to be neutral.	*Stated Commitment* In which the teacher always makes known his/her views during discussion.	It can stifle classroom discussion, inhibiting pupils from arguing a line against that of the teacher's. It may encourage some pupils to argue strongly for something they don't believe in simply because it's different from the teacher. Pupils often find it difficult to distinguish facts from values. It's even more difficult if the purveyor of facts and values is the same person, i.e. the teacher.

Essential: I think one of the main functions of a humanities or social studies teacher is to show that issues are hardly ever black and white. Necessary when the class is polarized on an issue. Most useful when dealing with issues about which there is a great deal of conflicting information. If a balanced range of opinion does not emerge from the group, then it is up to the teacher to see that the other aspects are brought out.	*A Balanced Approach* In which the teacher presents pupils with a wide range of alternative views.	Is there such a thing as a balanced range of opinions? As a strategy it has limited use. It avoids the main point by conveying the impression that 'truth' is a grey area that exists between two alternative sets of opinions. Balance means very different things to different people. The BBC's view of balance is not mine. Teaching is rarely value-free. This approach can lead to very teacher-directed lessons. Like BBC interviews you are always chipping in to maintain the so-called balance.
Frequently used by me. Great fun, and can be very effective in stimulating the pupils to contribute to discussion. Essential when faced by a group who all seem to share the same opinion. Most classes which I have taught seem to have a majority line. Then I use this strategy and parody, exaggeration, and role reversal. I often use this as a device to liven things up when the discussion is beginning to dry up.	*The Devil's Advocate Strategy* In which the teacher consciously takes up the **opposite** position to the one expressed by pupils or in teaching materials.	I have run into all sorts of problems with this approach. Kids identifying me with the views I was putting forward as devil's advocate; parents worried about my alleged views, etc. It may reinforce pupils' prejudices. Only to be used when discussion dries up and there are still 25 minutes left.

Classroom dilemmas

One of the basic themes of this book has been that no one teaching strategy is likely to prove successful in all circumstances. Instead we have advocated an eclectic and flexible approach which takes into account:

-the knowledge, values and experiences which the students bring with them into the classroom;

-the teaching methods which predominate in other lessons;

-the classroom climate (e.g. unquestioning consensus, apathy or polarization of opinion);

-the age and ability of the students;

-the reactions of pupils both to the content of lessons and the teaching methods being employed.

This general approach typifies much of the good practice we have observed. However, the best guide to good practice, in our view, is how a teacher handles what we have referred to as classroom dilemmas. They include highly emotional discussions, polarization of opinion and consequent hostility within the class, expression of extreme prejudices, unquestioning consensus, apathy and low motivation to participate, bullying of dissenting minorities, and so forth. Some are dilemmas which relate to specific types of controversial issue, some are dilemmas which essentially have implications for classroom management and yet other dilemmas arise out of pupil–teacher interaction.

A selection of these dilemmas is reproduced in the chart. We posed them to a group of teachers and found in their responses four basic procedures which can be classified as follows:

i) *Distancing procedures* When an issue proves highly sensitive within the community (e.g. teaching about Northern Ireland in the province itself; or teaching about law and order in a community with a recent history of unrest, protest and poor relations with the police, etc.) or when an issue generates a great deal of feeling or the class becomes polarized, teachers often seek temporarily to distance the discussion from the specific issue. This is done usually by breaking off to examine analogies and parallels, (e.g. Cyprus with Northern Ireland, or the treatment of teenagers who dress to be different with the treatment of minority groups), or they go back in time and trace the history of the issue under discussion.

ii) *Compensatory procedures* These are often employed when students are expressing strongly-held attitudes based on ignorance, or when the minority is bullied or discriminated against by the majority, or when there is unquestioning consensus. In such circumstances some teachers either take a more directive role— by playing devil's advocate, or highlighting contradictions in students' responses, or demythologizing policy statements—or they place the onus on students to consider points of view other than their own. This is done by either drawing up 'for and against' lists or by role reversal (working in a group to construct an argument against the position they would normally espouse).

iii) *Empathetic procedures* which are often turned to when the issue involves a group which is unpopular with some or all of the students, or when the issue involves covert discrimination against a particular group (e.g. sexism) or the issue is remote from students' own lives. Methods here usually include some of those already discussed above, including role reversals and for-and-against lists, but also role play and simulations and the

Some 'classroom dilemmas': What would you do?

---

1   The current topic on the syllabus is *Capital Punishment* and the group you are teaching are all strongly in favour of its reintroduction.

2   Imagine you are teaching in a multi-racial school and some of the white pupils in your class sympathize openly with the aims of the National Front. When you tell them you are going to show a filmstrip on *Immigration* from the Celts onwards, a few say that it is bound to be biased.

3   In a discussion of twentieth-century history a small group of pupils who are active members of CND bring up the question of *Nuclear Disarmament*; the rest appear uninterested.

4   After a series of recent bomb attacks, claimed by the Provisional IRA, pupils discuss with some fervour whether the troops should be brought out of *Northern Ireland*—emotions are running high.

5   There has been some recent controversy amongst the teaching staff about the use of *Corporal Punishment* in the school. This has filtered through to the local newspaper and after reading an article entitled 'Caning row rages in school!' pupils in your class want to discuss the issue.

6   Following a slide/tape presentation on the Third World, you try to get a discussion underway focusing on points raised in the film. It soon becomes apparent that the entire class are ignorant about the *Third World* but have strong attitudes about Britain's aid programme.

7   You attempt to start a discussion on the policies of the main parties for dealing with *Inflation*; this is greeted with loud yawns from some of the pupils and a generally apathetic response.

8   After a clash between youngsters and the police in the locality of the school, some pupils raise the question of *Police Harassment*, saying that the police cause most of the trouble.

9   During the recent dispute concerning teachers and employers when supervision was withdrawn, a few pupils raise the issue of whether this action was fair during a lesson on *Trade Unionism*. They want to know your views.

---

       use of vicarious experience through films, novels, comics and plays.

iv)   *Exploratory procedures* which are most commonly employed when the issue is not clearly defined (as is often the case with issues in the local community, or complex issues like law and order) or where the teacher's aim is not only to develop understanding of a specific issue but also analytical skills and knowledge of how to influence or change situations. In these cases the use of field work in the local community, projects, analysis of a number of real case studies and experience of parallel situations and problems (through role play and simulation) enable the students to explore the wider implications of an issue and possibly practise transferable skills.

Epilogue

Teaching controversial issues so that pupils should better understand the world they live in is a worthwhile aim in itself. However, if it is also possible to teach pupils certain process skills and ways of looking at issues which they themselves can transfer from one issue to another, then so much the better. We conclude therefore with some brief suggestions about the kinds of processes that might usefully be acquired by pupils. Essentially they can be categorized under four main headings:

> critically diagnosing information and evidence
> asking awkward questions
> recognizing rhetoric
> cultivating tentativeness.

1   *Critically diagnosing information and evidence*
> −Appreciating the complexity of an issue (i.e. not reducing it to simple dichotomies, black and white terms, etc.);
> −sorting out the arguments of the various groups and individuals involved;
> −sorting out relevant from irrelevant background information;
> −knowing potential sources of information and how to tap them;
> −recognizing the gaps in information supplied;
> −recognizing the limitations of the information provided;
> −evaluating the likely biases of the people supplying the information;
> −sorting out the similarities and differences in various accounts of an issue;
> −handling conflicting evidence or accounts of what has happened.

2   *Asking awkward questions* about public statements, newspaper articles, film and broadcasting commentaries by politicians, journalists, pressure group representatives and any other interested parties involved in a controversial issue:

> −What motives might these people have for supporting this point of view?
> −In what ways might they benefit from a particular solution, policy or argument being adopted?
> −What causes do they attribute to the present situation or dispute?
> −What relevant information has been or appears to have been omitted from the statement, article, film, etc?
> −What motives, if any, might they have for intentionally omitting this information?
> −Do they emphasize some points and play down others in their argument? Why might they do this?
> −What solutions, policies or recommendations, if any, are proposed to resolve this issue?

—Are there any solutions which have been overlooked?
—What reasons might they have for not considering these other solutions?
—What assumptions appear to be underlying their arguments?
—What is the factual basis of these assumptions? What would they need to prove or justify in order to substantiate these assumptions?
—What assumptions do you make when examining issues? Can you justify your own point of view?

Asking such questions is probably more important than always being able to find the answers.

3   *Recognizing rhetoric*
For example:

—use of false analogies;
—limitations of appeals to 'the lessons of history';
—uses of emotive language to gain support;
—appeals to the prejudice of the listener;
—use of diversionary tactics (e.g. restating the question, begging the question, casting doubt on the speaker's competence to speak rather than his/her arguments, etc.).

4   *'Cultivating tentativeness'*
Most teachers when teaching controversial issues will have experienced that moment when they seem to come up against a blank wall of unquestioned assumptions about the world. Marjorie Kraus, Vice President of the Close-Up Foundation in the United States, in describing her organization's programme of bringing 17,000 young Americans to Washington each year to see the political system in operation, emphasized that she and her colleagues were in the business of 'cultivating tentativeness'. She hoped that students who arrived in Washington with fixed ideas and prejudices would leave feeling less certain of their opinions. One of the teachers responding to our enquiry about teaching methods phrased it slightly differently:

> Often the result of teaching a topic is not 'clearer ideas' but 'greater confusion'. This has to be tolerated as a stage in moving towards an independent opinion.

In our view the litmus test of teaching controversial issues ought to be whether pupils who complete the course or unit of lessons are more likely to question their own and other people's assumptions and points of view.

References and bibliography

Chapter One

1 R. F. Dearden, 'Controversial issues in the curriculum', *Journal of Curriculum Studies*, v.13 n.1 (1981), pp 37–44.
2 C. Bailey, 'Neutrality and rationality in teaching' in D. Bridges and P. Scrimshaw (eds), *Values and Authority in Schools* (Hodder & Stoughton, London, 1975).
3 D. Fraser, *Deciding What to Teach* (NEA, Washington DC, 1963).
4 L. Stenhouse, *The Humanities Curriculum Project: An Introduction* (Heinemann, London, 1970).
5 H. J. Miller, 'The effectiveness of teaching techniques for reducing colour prejudice', *Liberal Education* v.16 (1969), pp 25–31.
6 James Cameron, 'Where Truth Lies', *The Guardian*, 16.11.82.
7 Stenhouse, 'Controversial Values Issues' in W. Carr (ed), *Values in the Curriculum* (NEA, Washington DC, 1970), pp 103–115.
8 L. Stenhouse and G. K. Verma, 'Educational Procedures and Attitudinal Objectives: A Paradox', *Journal of Curriculum Studies*, v.13 (1981), pp 329-337.
9 See, for example, I. A. Snook, *Indoctrination and Education* (Routledge & Kegan Paul, London, 1975).

Chapter Two

1 Robert Stradling, *The Political Awareness of the School Leaver* (Hansard Society, London, 1977), p 22.
2 Glasgow University Media Group, *Really Bad News* (Writers & Readers, London, 1982), p 142.
3 *New Society*, 24.9.81, p 20.
4 Denis Shemilt, *History 13-16: Evaluation Study* (Holmes McDougall, Edinburgh, 1980)' pp 7–8, 19, 81–2.
5 Schools Council *History 13-16 Project*, 'The Irish Question: Teachers' Guide' (Holmes McDougall, Edinburgh, 1977), p 6.
6 Schools Council *History 13-16 Project*, 'The Irish Question' (Holmes McDougall, Edinburgh, 1977).

7 David Lusted, 'Media Education and the Secondary/FE curriculum' in *Media Education Conference 1981: A Report*, British Film Institute Education (1982), p 20.

8 John Hartley, *Understanding News* (Methuen, London, 1982), pp 111–112.

9 For example, Campaign for Free Speech on Ireland, *The British Media and Ireland—Truth: The First Casualty*, from 1 Northend Road, London W14. See also P. Schlesinger in *Putting Reality Together* (Constable, London); and also the Glasgow University Media Group; **2**.

10 For example, see the British Film Institute's pack, *Reading Pictures* (BFI, London, 1981). See also *Camera Work*, Half Moon Photographs Workshop, 27 Alie Street, London E1; The Society for Education in Film and Television (SEFT) also distribute a number of exercises in editing visual material, available from 29 Old Compton Street, London W1V 5PL.

11 Northern Ireland Schools Cultural Studies Project, *Ulster: A Divided Society, Unit 5a*, p 18. This, and other Units, can be obtained from The Teachers' Centre, New University of Ulster, Coleraine, Northern Ireland.

12 Adapted from *The Troubles* edited by Taylor Downing (Thames Macdonald, London, 1980).

13 Northern Ireland Schools Cultural Studies Project, *Unit 5b*.

14 Eamon McCann, *War and an Irish Town* (Penguin Books, Harmondsworth, 1974).

15 First published in *The Daily Mirror*, 1.3.83, and adapted from A. F. N. Clarke, *Contact* (Secker & Warburg, London, 1983).

Chapter Three

1 Cited in A. G. Watts, 'The implications of School Leaver Unemployment for Careers Education in Schools', *Journal of Curriculum Studies*, v.10 n.3 (1978).

2 Training Services Agency, *Vocational Preparation for Young People* (MSC, London, 1975), p 15.

3 M. Levy, *YOP Survey*, West Midlands Regional Curriculum Unit/FEU, Birmingham 1980.

4 B. Hopson and M. Scally, *Lifeskills Teaching* (McGraw Hill, London, 1981), p 23.

5 National Economic Development Office, *Engineering Craftsmen: Strategies and Related Problems* (HMSO, London, 1977).

6 Dept. of Education and Science, *Careers Education in Secondary Schools*, Education Survey 18 (HMSO, London, 1973).

7 Dept. of Employment, Statistics Division, Orphanage Road, Watford, Herts SD1 1PJ.

8 See e.g. D. Massey and R. Meegan, *The Anatomy of Job Loss* (Methuen, London, 1982).

9 Source: Birmingham Community Development Project, *Workers on the Scrapheap* (London and Oxford, 1977), p 30.

10 L. Gow and A. McPherson (eds), *Tell Them From Me* (Aberdeen University Press, 1980).

11 C. Allinson and J. Harrison, *Youth Unemployment in Birmingham* (Young Volunteer Force Foundation, 1975).

12 R. E. Pahl, 'Living Without a Job: how school leavers see the future', *New Society*, 2.11.78, pp 259–262.

13 J. Daly and A. Roberts, *Rights Game Kit*, from Small Heath Community Law Centre, 477 Coventry Road, Small Heath, Birmingham B10 0TJ (1980).

14 National Youth Bureau, *Under 18*, from 17–23 Albion Street, Leicester LE1 6GD (1977).

15 R. Leach, *Coping with the System – A Brief Citizen's Manual* (National Extension College, 1980).

16 Community Service Volunteers, *The Survival Game*, from 237 Pentonville Road, London N1 9NJ.

Chapter Four

1 For an account of the development of this policy in Clissold Park School (now Stoke Newington School) see Jane Leggett 'Urgent Voices' in *The English Magazine*, n.9 (1982). These developments were stimulated by the report 'Developing Anti-Sexist Initiatives' (DASI), the outcome of a project funded by the Equal Opportunities Commission and the ILEA, 1981–2.

2 Judith Stinton, *Racism and Sexism in Children's Books* (Writers & Readers, London, 1979).

3 David Hicks, *Minorities* (Heinemann, London, 1981).

4 See for instance those reported in Dale Spender and Elizabeth Sarah (eds) *Learning to Lose* (The Women's Press, London, 1980); and Rosemary Deem (ed) *Schooling for Women's Work* (Routledge & Kegan Paul, London, 1980).

5 DES figures taken from *Promotion and the Woman Teacher*, Equal Opportunities Commission and the National Union of Teachers, 1980.

6 See Sara Delamont, *Sex Roles in Schools* (Methuen, London, 1980); similar findings were noted by the team on the *Girls Into Science and Technology* (GIST) project, based at Manchester Polytechnic, 1979–83.

7 Barbara Ludlow, Greenwich Local History Library. Report from the Conference *Developing Anti-Sexist Approaches in History and Social Sciences*, 1982 at the History and Social Sciences Teachers' Centre, 377 Clapham Road, London SW9 9BT.

8 Carol Adams, Paula Bartley, Judy Lown & Cathy Loxton, *Under Control* (Cambridge University Press, 1983). See also Ivy Pinchbeck, *Women Workers in the Industrial Revolution* (Virago 1981); Alice Clark, *Working Life of Women in the Seventeenth Century* (RKP 1982).

9 Carol Adams and Rae Lauriekietis, *The Gender Trap* (3 volumes) (Quartet, 1975–76). Jean Coussins, *Taking Liberties: A Teaching Pack for Boys and Girls on Equal Rights* (Virago 1979).

10   See booklist by Carol Adams and Diana Hargreave, *Her Studies: A Resources List for Teachers of History and Social Science*, from the ILEA History and Social Sciences Teachers' Centre, 377 Clapham Road, London SW9, and from the Schools Council.

Chapter Five

1   Ian Lister, 'Political Socialization and the schools', *Teaching Politics*, 2 (1973).
2   T. S. Bowles, *Survey of Attitudes Towards Overseas Development* (Central Office of Information, London, 1978).
3   Department of Education and Science, *Education in Schools* (HMSO, London, 1977).
4   Dudley Seers, *Bulletin of the Institute of Development Studies*, October 1975.
5   Dudley Seers, *Development Options* (IDS Discussion Paper n.165, Sussex, 1981).
6   Shridath Ramphal, quoted in *Crisis Decade: The World in the Eighties* (International Coalition for Development Action, 1980), p 2.
7   Mary Worrall, 'Multiracial Britain and the Third World: tensions and approaches in the classroom', *The New Era*, 59 (1978), p 49.
8   See e.g. J. L. Hodge *et al*, *Cultural Bases of Racism and Group Oppression* (Two Riders Press, California, 1975).
9   N. Annan, *Report of the Committee on the Future of Broadcasting* (HMSO, Cmnd 6753, London 1977).
10   Birmingham Development Education Centre, *Priorities for Development* (Birmingham, 1982) p 2.
11   Michael Storm, 'Studies of distant environments in primary schools: some problems', *Teachers' World*, Summer 1971.
12   Ann Hurman, *As Others See Us* (Edward Arnold, London, 1977).
13   P. Jones *et al*, *Development Studies: A Handbook for Teachers* (SOAS, London, 1977).
14   R. Tiffen, *Communication and Politics* (Australia, 1975).
15   See, for example, R. Tames, *Emergent Nations* and *Case Studies of Emergent Nations* (both published by Blackie, Glasgow, 1981); N. Taylor and R. Richardson, *Change & Choice*, from the Centre For World Development Education (CWDE), 128 Buckingham Palace Road, London SW1; Northants Development Education Project, *Development Strategies*, also from CWDE; John Bale, *Patterns of Underdevelopment* (Nelson, London, 1982); J. S. Stuart, *The Unequal Third* (Edward Arnold, 1977); John Turner, *World Inequality* (Longman, 1978).
16   World Studies Project, *Learning for Change in World Society* (CWDE, 1976).
17   For more ideas on teaching abstract concepts see Taylor and Richardson, *Change & Choice*; and the booklets, particularly *Conflict* and *Interdependence* produced by the *Jordanhill Project on International Understanding*, from Jordanhill College of Education, Southbrae Drive, Glasgow G13 1PP.

Chapter Six

1 See *Report and Final Document* from the United Nations Educational, Scientific and Cultural Organization World Congress on Disarmament Education, Paris, 1980.

2 Rick Rodgers, 'Peace Studies', *Where* n.121, pp 14–17, September 1982.

3 For example, *Huntingdon Post*, 28.4.83; *The Teacher*, 29.4.83.

4 Reported in *The Times Educational Supplement*, 18.3.83.

5 Reported in *The Guardian* and *The Sun* (among others), 28.3.83.

6 *The Sun*, 29.3.83.

7 The concept of 'doemdenken' (doom-thinking) has become so widespread in the Netherlands that the word is in general use and much concern is being expressed. This is discussed by Jan de Jong in a paper 'Teaching About Nuclear Weapons', presented to the Atlantic College Peace Studies project conference, June 1981.

8 Robin Richardson, 'Justice and Equality in the Classroom—the Design of Lessons and Courses', occasional paper number *WSDS/7* for the World Studies Teacher Training Centre, University of York, 1982, p1.

9 Adam Suddaby, *Nuclear Weapons and Warfare* (in six booklets) (Longman, Harlow, 1983).

10 Colin Lacey and Pauline Jan, *An Issue to Debate: The Nuclear Question* (Tressell Publications, 1981).

11 Nikki Haydon and Jim Mulligan, *Nuclear Issues*, Thames Television 1983 (to accompany their series of four programmes on *The English Programme*, May 1983).

12 *The Arms Trade Game*, Campaign Against the Arms Trade.

13 *Finger On The Button*, published by *The New Internationalist*.

14 UNICEF: *An Approach to Peace Education*, School Series n.6, Development Education.

Chapter Seven

1 Robert Stradling, *The Political Awareness of the School Leaver* (Hansard Society, 1977).

2 Eileen Wormald, 'Apolitical women: the myth of early socialization', *International Journal of Political Education*, v.6 (1983), pp 43–64.

3 D. Hamingson (ed), *Towards Judgement:* the publications of the Evaluation Unit of the Humanities Curriculum Project, 1970–72, Occasional Publications, n.1 (Norwich Centre for Applied Research in Education).